THE EASTERN ORTHODOX CHURCH

THE EASTERN ORTHODOX CHURCH

ITS THOUGHT AND LIFE

Ernst Benz

AldineTransaction
A Division of Transaction Publishers
New Brunswick (U.S.A.) and London (U.K.)

New paperback printing 2009
Copyright © 1957 by Rowohlt Taschenbuch Verlag.

This book is printed on acid-free paper that meets the American National Standard for Permanence of Paper for Printed Library Materials.

Library of Congress Catalog Number: 2008027239
ISBN: 978-0-202-36298-4
Printed in the United States of America

Library of Congress Cataloging-in-Publication Data

Benz, Ernst, 1907-1978.
   [Geist und Leben der Ostkirche. English]
   The Eastern Orthodox Church : its thought and life / Ernst Benz.
      p. cm.—(Anchor)
   Originally published: Garden City, N.Y. : Anchor Books, 1963. (Anchor)
   Includes bibliographical references and index.
   ISBN 978-0-202-36298-4 (alk. paper)
     1. Orthodox Eastern Church.   I. Title.

BX320.3.B4613 2008
281.9—dc22
                                               2008027239

Contents

THE EASTERN ORTHODOX CHURCH

I.

The Orthodox Icon

The non-Orthodox western European finds it most difficult
to comprehend the Eastern Orthodox Church because he
knows little about the life and doctrines of Orthodoxy and
even this little is overlaid by many strata of prejudices and
misunderstandings, partly religious, partly political in nature. One of the stumbling blocks to our understanding of
Orthodoxy has been our natural tendency to confound the
ideas and customs of the Orthodox Church with familiar
parallels in Roman Catholicism. To escape these traditional
misunderstandings and prejudices, we will not follow the
usual course of textbooks, which for the most part begin by
outlining the doctrines of the Orthodox Church. Such a
procedure almost inevitably leaves the student to equate
these with the forms of western Christianity.

Since ours is so markedly visual an era, another approach seems wiser: the appeal to the eye, to pictorial
perception. This is all the more logical an approach to
the Eastern Orthodox Church because this church gives a
central place to icons,[1] or holy images. It is only in the

---

[1] *eikon* (Greek) = picture.

past few decades that western Europe has discovered this branch of art. Nevertheless, through it many persons who had no conception of the Orthodox Church have received a direct impression of an important aspect of Orthodox piety. We have had numerous art books on Eastern icon painting. Magnificent exhibitions of icons have been arranged in Germany, France, England and Italy, through which Westerners have had the opportunity to see and study the nature and history of icon painting. Icon painting, then, will be our point of departure for an introduction to the life and thought of the Eastern Orthodox Church.

1. THE ROLE OF ICONS IN ORTHODOX PIETY

Any Western observer of an Orthodox service will immediately notice the special importance the pictures of saints have for the Orthodox believer. The Orthodox believer who enters his church to attend services first goes up to the iconostasis, the wall of paintings which separates the sanctuary from the nave. There he kisses the icons in a definite order: first the Christ icons, then the Mary icons, then the icons of the angels and saints. After this he goes up to a lectern—*analogion*—placed in front of the iconostasis. On this lectern the icon of the saint for the particular day or the particular church feast is displayed. Here, too, he pays his respects by a kiss, bow and crossing himself. Then having expressed his veneration for the icons, he steps back and rejoins the congregation.

This veneration of icons takes place not only in the church, but also at home. Every Orthodox family has an icon hanging in the eastern corner of the living room and bedroom, the so-called "beautiful" corner. It is customary for a guest, upon entering a room, to greet the icons first by crossing himself and bowing. Only then does he greet his host.

To apprehend the special significance of the saint's image in the Eastern Orthodox Church we must consider the iconoclastic struggle. The anti-image movement was as passionate as the campaign later to be led by Luther and Calvin for purifying and reforming the western branch of the Catholic Church. During the eighth and ninth centuries —partly through the influence of Islamic rationalism—an opposition to images began to pervade the Byzantine Church, led chiefly by a number of rationalistic Byzantine emperors (Leo III, the Isaurian, 716–41; Constantine V Copronymus, 741–75; Leo IV, 775–80; Leo V, the Armenian, 813–20; Theophilus, 829–42). This attack upon the sacred images shook the whole of Orthodox Christendom to its foundations. Although the instruments of political power were in the hands of the iconoclasts, who upheld their cause by burning images, by exiling and imprisoning the opposite party, their point of view was not victorious. The struggle ended ultimately in the reestablishment of the veneration of images. The "Feast of Orthodoxy," which the entire Orthodox Church celebrates annually, was instituted in the year 842 to honor the victory of the iconophiles and the Church's official restoration of image-veneration under the Empress Theodora.

2. THE "STRANGENESS" OF ICONS

The Western observer will be struck by the style of these icons, as well as by the reverence shown to them. They have a curious archaic strangeness which partly fascinates, partly repels him. This strangeness is not easy to describe. When we of the West admire a painting, we admire it as the creative achievement of a particular artist. This is true even of religious art. A Madonna by Raphael is to us first of all a creative work of Raphael. Although sacred persons such as Christ, Mary, or the apostles are for the most part represented according to traditional concepts, the individual painter is concerned with giving the picture his personal stamp, and displaying his creative imagination. The painting of the Eastern Church, on the other hand, lacks precisely this element of free creative imagination which we prize. Centuries and centuries have passed in which the painters of the Eastern Church have been content to repeat certain types of sacred images. We do, of course, find certain variations between centuries and between the styles of different countries; but when we set these against the enormous range of style within the art of the Western Church, the deviations appear very slight, sometimes barely discernible. It is usually impossible for anyone but a specialist to assign an icon of the Eastern Church to any specific century. Knowledge of the art of the West is no help at all. For the art of the Eastern Church has nothing corresponding to the various styles into which the course of Western art can be divided, such as Romanesque, Gothic, Renaissance.

Thus, since we take our own standards for granted, we are apt to try to judge icon painting by our Western conceptions of religious art. We will then come to highly negative conclusions; we may decide that the ecclesiastical art of the Eastern Orthodox Church entirely lacks creative originality, or that its attachment to tradition is a sign of artistic incompetence. We must, however, cast aside such preconceptions and try to see these icons in the framework of their own culture.

The Eastern Church takes quite another view of the role of the individual artist. Most of the Orthodox ecclesiastical painters have remained anonymous. Moreover, an icon painting is not the work of an "artist," as we understand the word. Rather, the making of icons is a sacred craft and is practiced in monasteries that have won a reputation for this work. Each monastery represents a certain school. But these schools are not built around some outstanding painter who has communicated a new creative impulse to his disciples. Rather, the school is based on a tradition that is carefully preserved and passed on from one generation of monks to the next. Icons are often group products, each monk attending to his own specialty. One paints the eyes, another the hair, a third the hands, a fourth the robes, so that even in the productive process itself the factor of creative, artistic individuality is eliminated.

In order to understand the painting of the Eastern Church the Occidental observer must make a certain effort of will; he must stop comparing icons to Western forms of painting and attempt to grasp the peculiar nature of Eastern icon making in terms of its theological justifications. To do this, he must be clear about certain fundamental matters.

3. THE DOGMATIC NATURE OF ICONS

The art of icon painting cannot be separated from the ecclesiastical and liturgical functions of the icons. Many Orthodox believers consider it sheer blasphemy to exhibit icons in a museum. To them this is a profanation. For the icon is a sacred image, a consecrated thing. This fact is present from the beginning, even as the icon is made. The procedure of painting itself is a liturgical act, with a high degree of holiness and sanctification demanded of the painter. The painter-monks prepare themselves for their task by fasting and penances. Brushes, wood, paints, and all the other necessary materials are consecrated before they are used. All this only confirms the theory that the sacred image has a specific spiritual function within the Eastern Orthodox Church, and that its tradition-bound form springs not from any lack of skill but from specific theological and religious conceptions which prohibit any alteration of the picture.

4. THE THEOLOGY OF ICONS

During the eighth and ninth centuries, when the great battle over the icons was raging, the Fathers of the Byzantine Church wrote quantities of tracts in defense of sacred images. A glance at this literature is most instructive.

Thus we see that from the very first the Orthodox theologians did not interpret icons as products of the creative imagination of a human artist. They did not consider them works of men at all. Rather, they regarded them as manifestations of the heavenly archetypes. Icons, in their view, were a kind of window between the earthly and the celestial worlds—a window through which the inhabitants of the celestial world looked down into ours and on which the true features of the heavenly archetypes were imprinted two-dimensionally. The countenance of Christ, of the Blessed Virgin, or of a saint on the icons was therefore a true epiphany, a self-made imprint of the celestial archetypes. Through the icons the heavenly beings manifested themselves to the congregation and united with it.

Several iconologists of the eighth and ninth centuries developed this conception into the idea of incarnation: in the icon Christ becomes incarnate in the very materials, that is, in wood, plaster, egg white and oil, just as he incarnated in flesh and blood when he became a man. This idea never gained acceptance as Orthodox dogma. Nevertheless Orthodox theology does teach that the icons reproduce the archetypes of the sacred figures in the celestial world. Along with this goes an express prohibition against three-dimensional images of the saints. The celestial figures manifest themselves exclusively upon the mirror surface or window surface of the icon. The golden background of the icon represents the heavenly aura that surrounds the saints. To look through the window of the icon is to look straight into the celestial world. The two-dimensionality of the icon, therefore, and its golden nimbus are intimately bound up with its sacred character.

5. THE ICON "NOT MADE BY HANDS"

This conception of the icon as epiphany or "appearance" is fundamentally strange to us. We may approach an understanding of it if we bear in mind that many icons of the

Eastern Church, especially the icons of Christ himself, are traditionally ascribed to archetypes "not made by hands." These are pictures that appeared by some miracle—as, for example, the picture Christ left of himself when, according to an ancient legend of the Church, he sent to King Abgar of Edessa the linen cloth with which he had dried his face, upon which his portrait was impressed. This cloth with its picture "not made by hands" afterward worked many miracles. Other Christ icons are attributed to Luke, the painter among the apostles, who is credited by Orthodox tradition with having painted the first portraits of Jesus in his embodiment as man. Numerous icons of Mary also "appeared" in miraculous fashion: either the Blessed Virgin personally appeared in a church and left her picture behind as visible proof of the genuineness of her appearance or else an icon "painted itself" miraculously.

A favorite legend of the Eastern Church is that of the holy icon painter Alypios, who attained to such holiness by his praying and fasting that the saints themselves took over the work of painting for him and miraculously limned themselves on the wooden tablets that he had prepared for painting. Much of the legend consists of stories describing how the painter is prevented from painting by illness or the malice of enemies. But on the day that the commissioned icon is supposed to be ready, it is found finished "of its own accord," even though the painter had been physically unable to work on it. The saint who was to be represented on the icon suddenly appears, surrounded with wonderful light, steps into the empty surface of the wood and leaves behind his "authentic" image. A supernatural light long continues to emanate from the icon, thus confirming the miraculous personal entrance of the archetype into the image.

Only by keeping this idea constantly in mind will we be able to grasp the special nature of Eastern Orthodox icon painting. Its repetitive quality was not due to a deficiency of artistic imagination. By the very nature of the icon, any intervention of human imagination is excluded. To change an icon would be to distort the archetype, and any alteration of a celestial archetype would be heretical in the same sense as a willful alteration of ecclesiastical dogma.

6. ICON AND LITURGY

The direct relationship between icon and liturgy is of crucial importance. Orthodox liturgy reaches its height in the celebration of the Eucharist. Orthodox doctrine holds that in the Eucharist the congregation experiences the manifestation of Christ, the foretaste of *parousia*, the Second Coming of Christ in glory. What is more, in the Eucharist there takes place the meeting of the entire congregation of heaven with the earthly congregation. Within the sanctified space of the church, heaven descends upon earth when the Eucharist is celebrated. Christ enters as triumphant Lord, surrounded by choirs of cherubim and seraphim, "borne upon the spears of the Heavenly Hosts," as the liturgy puts it.

The images in the church represent this epiphany. In view of this, it becomes important that the holy images have their fixed places within the church. To each spot inside the church certain icons are assigned; above all, the sanctuary, the iconostasis and the dome are adorned. For example, the icons of the two saints who originated the two Eucharistic liturgies employed in the Eastern Church—St. John Chrysostom and St. Basil—belong in the prothesis,[2] the chapel to the left of the altar where the Eucharistic elements are prepared. The special meaning of the arrangement is even plainer on the screen, the iconostasis. To begin with, the iconostasis was a simple, low barrier that separated the sanctuary from the rest of the church. In the course of the centuries, however, and under the influence of iconography, it grew higher and higher until it became

[2] *Próthesis* (Gk.) = preparation.

a wall completely separating sanctuary from nave. This wall permits communication between the priest at the altar and the congregation only through three doors: the middle or royal door, a door on the right (south) and one on the left (north).

The icons are not scattered over the iconostasis, but arranged in a fixed order. For example, the icon of Christ is always to the right, beside the royal central door; to its left is the icon of the Mother of God; to the right of Christ, the icon of John the Baptist, and to the left of Mary, the icon of the saint to whom the church is dedicated. The archangels Gabriel and Michael are usually to be found on the door itself, as representatives of the highest choirs of the heavenly host. These are the principal icons and are usually life-size. Above them hang three or four rows of smaller icons—their number depending on the size of the church—in which the whole story of redemption and the hierarchy of the celestial Church are represented. The usual order is as follows: first a row of apostles, then a row of saints and martyrs, then a row of prophets, and finally a row of patriarchs of the Old Testament. Above the middle door there is usually the *deesis,* a representation of Christ on his throne as ruler of the universe, with Mary and John standing to his right and left, in poses indicating that they are interceding for men. Thus the succession of images presents to the congregation the whole of the celestial Church. The pictorial content of the iconostasis corresponds precisely to the theological content of the Eucharistic liturgy.

The icons carry out a liturgical function in still another manner. Each day, and especially each feast day, has its special icon. Thus, for Christmas the icon of the Nativity is brought out. These icons present believers with a picture of the sacred event which corresponds exactly with the established prayers and liturgical texts. For example, the Christmas liturgy—a body of venerable chants and prayers dating from the fourth to the ninth centuries—presents the traditional conception of the birth of Christ as taking place in a cave. The Christmas icons also set the scene of the Nativity in a cave. If the artist were allowed any latitude on this question and laid the scene—as Western painters do —in a stable, the mystical interpretations of the Nativity in the cave—interpretations in which the liturgy abounds— would suddenly lose validity. In this case as in so many others, the whole liturgical order of the Church depends upon the faithful reproduction of time-honored archetypes.

7. LITURGY AND THE CONSECRATION OF ICONS

Further evidence of the nature of the icon emerges from the procedure by which the priest dedicates a newly painted icon for service in a church. This act of consecration is absolutely essential, for it is the Church's confirmation of the identity between the painted picture and the celestial archetype. The liturgy used in present-day consecrations shows distinct traces of the conflicts that raged throughout the Church during the iconoclastic controversies of the eighth and ninth centuries. In those days the foes of icons appealed above all to the second of the Ten Commandments: "You shall not make yourself a graven image, or any likeness of anything" (Exodus 20:4). They insisted that the Orthodox Church's veneration of images was a flouting of God's explicit prohibition of images. Such veneration, they held, was at the expense of the reverence due to God alone.

The prayers and hymns used in the consecration of icons allude to both these arguments. The initial prayer stresses that in prohibiting images God was referring only to the making of idols: "By Thy Commandment Thou hast forbidden the making of images and likenesses which are repugnant to Thee, the true God, that they may not be worshiped and served as if they were the Lord." After this statement the prayer points out all the more emphatically that God himself commanded "setting up of images which do not glorify the name of strange, false and nonexistent gods, but glorify Thy all-holy and sublime Name, the Name of the only true God." Among such images the prayer mentions the Ark of the Covenant adorned with two golden cherubim and the cherubim of gold-covered cypress wood which God ordered to be installed upon Solomon's temple. Thus, after outlawing the idolatrous worship of false images, God began to depict the secrets of his kingdom in images. But God then performed the supreme act of self-portraiture—the liturgical prayer continues—by becoming flesh, by the incarnation in his Son, who is the "image of the invisible God" (Col. 1:15) and who "reflects the glory of God." God himself, "shaper of the whole of visible and invisible creation," shaped an image of himself in Jesus Christ, his perfect icon. Thus God himself was the first icon maker, making a visible reproduction of himself in Christ.

There now follows the most striking turn of phrase, and one that is most startling to western Europeans: the liturgy asserts that we have an image of Christ himself (who is the image of the Father), an image "not made by hands" which exactly reproduces the features of the God-man. The liturgy is referring to the miraculous image mentioned above which Christ sent to King Abgar of Edessa and also to the tradition of the cloth with which Christ dried his face on the way to Golgotha and which miraculously retained the imprint of his features. Christ himself, then, made the first Christ icon and thus legitimized both icon painting and the veneration of icons.

This argument disposes of the iconoclasts' first objection. Their second objection, that veneration of the holy images robs God of the honor due to him alone, is confuted by a second argument drawn from Neoplatonic speculation on the problem of images. "We do not deify the icons, but know that the homage paid to the image rises to the archetype." It is not the image which is the object or the recipient of veneration, but the archetype which "manifests itself" in it. In intercessory prayers, too, there is the parenthetic reminder that the images must not mislead anyone into withholding from God the veneration that is due to him alone as the archetype of all holiness.

8. PRINCIPAL TYPES OF ICONS
AND THEIR PLACE IN DOGMA

Christ Icons

A particular type of image, which came more and more into use during the fourth and fifth centuries in representations of the holy sudarium [handkerchief used in Roman times for wiping away sweat] led to the dogmatic fixation of the Christ icon. The model was found in an apocryphal document of the early Church, the so-called Epistle of Lentulus. Lentulus is mentioned in ancient historical records as having been consul during the twelfth year of the reign of Tiberius. In the epistle Lentulus is identified as a Roman official, Pontius Pilate's superior, who happens to be in Palestine at the time of Jesus' appearance there, and who makes an official report to the emperor. The official report also included a warrant for the arrest of Jesus which ran as follows:

"At this time there appeared and is still living a man—if indeed he may be called a man at all—of great powers named the Christ, who is called Jesus. The people term him the prophet of truth; his disciples call him Son of God, who wakens the dead and heals the sick—a man of erect stature, of medium height, fifteen and a half fists high, of temperate and estimable appearance, with a manner inspiring of respect, nut-brown hair which is smooth to the ears and from the ears downward shaped in gentle locks and flowing down over the shoulders in ample curls, parted in the middle after the manner of the Nazarenes, with an even and clear brow, a face without spots or wrinkles, and of healthy color, Nose and mouth are flawless; he wears a luxuriant beard of the color of his hair. He has a simple and mature gaze, large, blue-gray eyes that are uncommonly varied in expressiveness, fearsome when he scolds and gentle and affectionate when he admonishes. He is gravely cheerful, weeps often, but has never been seen to laugh. In figure he is upright and straight; his hands and arms are well shaped. In conversation he is grave, mild and modest, so that the word of the prophet concerning the 'fairest of the sons of men' (Ps. 45:2) can be applied to him."

The Byzantine Christ type is modeled after this description. He appears, however, in a number of different guises, depending on the aspect of Christ's nature which is being stressed: Christ as Lord of the universe (*Pantokrator*); Christ as Teacher and Preacher of the gospel; Christ as the Judge of the world, with stern countenance and "terrible eye."

Icons of the Holy Trinity

Unlike the Christ images, the picture of the Holy Trinity cannot be traced back to a miraculous self-portrait. Nevertheless, it too must follow a strict canon. The theologians of the early Church searched the Old Testament for references to the Trinity. They settled on a passage that, but for their exegeses, would scarcely seem to have this hidden meaning, at least to the modern mind. The passage deals with the visit of the three angels to Abraham in the grove of Mamre (Gen. 18:9 ff.). The theologians of the early Church took this visit to signify a manifestation of the Trinity. Thus the first type of Trinity icon in the Eastern Church depicts the three angels appearing to Abraham in the grove of Mamre.

A second type of Trinity icon depicts the Trinity as it is present at the baptism of Jesus. The Son stands in the waters of the Jordan; the Father is represented as a hand reaching down from heaven; and the Holy Spirit hovers above the Son in the form of a dove (Matt. 3:16–17). The New Testament yields two other pictures of the Trinity: the Pentecost scene, in which the Savior risen to heaven sits by the right hand of God, while the Holy Spirit, the "Comforter," is sent down to the apostles in the form of tongues of fire; and finally the vision on Mount Tabor, in which the Father reveals himself as a voice from heaven —once again represented by the outstretched hand—the Holy Spirit appears in the cloud, and the Son is shown transfigured by light, as he appeared to the three disciples.

There is a special formula with which these icons are consecrated. Both the Old Testament and the New Testament archetypes are invoked: "And as the Old Testament tells us of Thine appearance in the form of the three angels to the glorious patriarch Abraham, so in the New Testament the Father revealed himself in the voice, the Son in the flesh in the Jordan, but the Holy Spirit in the form of the dove. And the Son again, who rose to heaven in the flesh and sits by the right hand of God, sent the Comforter, the Holy Spirit, to the apostles in the form of tongues of fire. And upon Tabor the Father revealed himself in the voice; the Holy Spirit in the cloud; and the Son, in the brightest of all light, to the three disciples. So, for lasting remembrance, we profess Thee, sole God of our praise, we profess Thee not with our lips alone, but also paint Thy form, not to deify it, but so that seeing it with the eyes of the body we may look with the eyes of the spirit upon Thee, our God, and by venerating it we may praise and lift up Thee, our Creator, Redeemer and Uniter."

Icons of the Mother of God

The New Testament lacks any such direct dogmatic basis for the icons of Mary. The Mariology of the fourth century had to create such a basis. To supply the want, there arose numerous legends revolving about the miraculous appearances of miracle-working images of the Blessed Virgin. In many cases the Mother of God herself was supposed to have appeared on earth. As a sign of her visit she would leave behind an icon whose supernatural light would attract the attention of chance passersby. Or else some believer would have a vision in which the hiding place of a miraculous icon would be revealed. A large number of Orthodox monasteries and churches not only in Russia but in other Orthodox countries were founded on the spot hallowed by the discovery of some such icon "not made by hands."

All consecrations of icons end with a prayer addressed directly to the person represented in the icon. Thus at the end of the consecration of the Christ icon the priest prays: "He who once deigned to imprint upon the sweat-cloth the outline, not made by hands, of his perfectly pure and divine-human countenance, Christ our true God, mild lover of men, have mercy upon us and save us." Similarly at the close of the consecration of a Mary icon, these words are spoken: "We flee to Thy mercy, God-bearer; disdain not our cries of woe."

Icons of Saints

The liturgy of consecration for the icons of saints makes it plain that the saints themselves, in their turn, are regarded as images of Christ. The Orthodox Church venerates the saints as "the hands of God," by which he accomplishes his works in the Church; even after their deaths these saints perform works of love as intercessors and helpers and smooth their fellowmen's path to salvation. They are the earthly proof of the invisible celestial Church, whose purposes they implement. The Orthodox Church states explicitly that the saints do not obscure the greatness of Christ's person and works, but rather that all veneration offered to the saints returns to their archetype, Christ. The images of the saints are therefore reflections of the Christ image, which in turn is the renewal and perfection of the image of God implanted in the first man. Therefore the icons of saints are consecrated with the following formula: "Lord, our God, Thou who created man after Thine image and Thy likeness and, after this image was destroyed by the disobedience of the first created man, hast renewed it by the incarnation of Thy Christ, who assumed the form of a servant and became in appearance like unto a man, and whom Thou hast restored to the first dignity among Thy saints; in solemnly revering Thy icons, we revere the saints themselves, who are Thine image and Thy likeness. In venerating them we venerate and glorify Thee as their archetype."

Icons of Angels

Along with the figures of the Evangelists and saints, the images of angels have a prominent place in Orthodox iconography. This is in keeping with the position of angels in the doctrines of the Eastern Church. God or Christ never appears alone; the divine Persons are always surrounded by a crowd of the heavenly host divided into various choirs. Chief in the hierarchy of the celestial Church is the Archangel Michael, the prince of angels, who leads the heavenly hosts in the struggle against Satan and his followers, and drives them out of heaven. But the lesser angels are also favorite subjects of Orthodox iconography. At one point in the liturgy of the Eucharist, angels are supposed to enter the church and join the priests, the deacons and the congregation in singing the cherubim's hymn of praise, "Holy, Holy, Holy, Lord God of hosts" (Isaiah 6:3). Icons of angels as participants in the singing have their fixed liturgical place in the sanctuary as well as on the iconostasis.

Scenic Icons

Frequent subjects for icons are scenes and characters of the Old and New Testaments, which are the source of the principal Christian feasts, or important institutions of the Church. There are a whole series of icons relating to the monastic tradition. Scenes from the Old Testament are paired with scenes from the New Testament according to a fixed pattern of promise and fulfillment (see p. 30). Thus, for example, a favorite subject for icons is the prophet Elijah, who is considered the Old Testament prototype of

Christian monasticism, forefather of those wise ascetics who fought demons in the desert and performed miracle upon miracle. Another favorite is John the Baptist, who is shown dressed in his hair shirt and living in the desert.

These icons too conform strictly to liturgy. There is, for example, the so-called "Resurrection icon," which, however, does not illustrate the Resurrection of Christ as we understand it and as it has been painted by Dürer or Grüne-wald—Christ breaking open the tomb and emerging from it. Instead these icons depict Christ's descent into Hades; he is shown storming the innermost fortress of Satan, or breaking the bars of the gate to the underworld, or lifting the gates of Hades from their hinges. On one such "Resurrection icon" Christ is shown standing upon the gates of hell which he has lifted from their hinges and arranged in the form of a cross; from the interior emerge the souls of the devout of ancient times, led by Adam and Eve who having been first to fall are the first to be liberated from Hades. Behind the first parents come the just patriarchs, kings and pious fathers of the Old Testament, who have been waiting all this time for their redemption. These icons are the counterparts of the Easter hymns of the Eastern Church, which take Christ's journey to Hades as their subject.

Establishment of the Rules of Icon Painting

Iconography, therefore, cannot be considered apart from the total context of liturgy and dogma in the Orthodox Church. Its every detail is fixed by tradition and must conform to ecclesiastical requirements. This is true even for the colors. The very oldest writings of mystical theology (the writings that are ascribed to Dionysius the Areopagite —cf. Acts 17:34—though in fact they belong to the fifth century and were written by some unknown figure in Syria) contain an elaborate system of color symbolism; certain liturgical colors of the earthly Church are related to the colors of corresponding choirs of angels in the celestial hierarchy, and each of the colors is given specific spiritual

and moral significances on the basis of its celestial archetype. This tradition of color symbolism was retained in the
Orthodox Church and found its way into the monastic man-
uals on painting. Hence even the coloration of the icons was
not left to the imagination of the monastic icon painters, for
every color had a symbolic significance. Thus the garments
of certain saints always had to be painted in prescribed
colors that were in keeping with their spiritual character.

On this score too we can no longer say that the rigidity
of icon painting resulted from the meager creative powers
of the artists. The very quality that we Westerners expect
of them was strictly forbidden by their Church. These Eastern painters adhered to the traditional forms prescribed by
the Church not because they could do no better, but because for their souls' salvation they did not dare do otherwise, and because they thought of themselves as humble
copyists of celestial archetypes. Thus the iconography of
the Eastern Church keeps alive a kind of primitive script
used to record archetypal religious experience. It is an art
that goes back to the earliest age of the Church, when the
power of visionary insight was as yet unbroken.

Icons and Dogma

When we understand the importance of icons in Orthodox worship, we are better prepared to understand the
Orthodox religious system, for the concept of icons themselves is a central point of dogma which crops up again
and again in all aspects of Orthodox theology. The idea of
the image has its counterpart in the relationship between
man and God. Man is created "in the image of God"; he
carries the icon of God within himself. This belief is so
central to Orthodox theology and anthropology, the consciousness that man was imprinted with the image of God
from the day of creation is so dominant, that the idea of
original sin never could become established within the
Orthodox Church in its blunt Western form. Sin manifests
itself as a distortion, a damaging, infecting and tainting of

the image of God; but it cannot rob man of his original nobility. This is always his because he remains the image of God.

This image-concept also dominates the Christology and the doctrine of the Trinity in the Eastern Church. The divine Logos is the image of the Father, in which he first took form, the "stamp of his nature," the "radiance of his glory" (Heb. 1:3). The work of redemption by the incarnate Logos, who is an image of the heavenly Father and in whom "the whole fullness of deity dwells" (Col. 2:9), consists in renewing the image of God which the first man stained by sin. Christ is the "new Adam" in whom the original image of God of the old Adam is restored. The whole meaning of redemption, then, is linked with this concept of image; the redemption of man consists in man's being renewed in the image of Jesus Christ, incorporated into the image of Christ and thus through Jesus Christ experiencing the renewal of his status as image of God.

The role of the Church is also defined in terms of the image. The Church exists so that its many members may be incorporated into the image of Jesus Christ, the "perfect man" (Eph. 4:12), in that the individual believers are "changed into his likeness" (2 Cor. 3:18). Thus Orthodox theology holds up the icon as the true key to the understanding of Orthodox dogma.

II.

Liturgy and Sacraments

1. THE LITURGY

The Celestial Wedding Supper in the Preaching of Jesus

In order to understand the spirit of this liturgy, we must go back to the very beginnings of Christian worship. Before Jesus appeared on the scene, Judaism was in the grip of a fervent expectation of the kingdom of God that was to be ushered in and accomplished by the appearance of the Messiah and Son of Man. These hopes for the coming of the kingdom of God were not couched in terms of theological abstractions: they were hopes of something quite definite and tangible, of a joyous new state of existence. Again and again this hope was expressed in terms of the image of the Messianic meal: the glory to come "sitting down" (literally: lying at table) in the kingdom of God. "Blessed is he who shall eat bread in the kingdom of God" (Luke 14:15).

In his sermon on the kingdom of God, Jesus gave a new content to this anticipation. Once more we come upon the metaphor of the Messianic meal, of blissfully lying at table with the raised-up Messiah-Son-of-Man. "And they shall come from the east, and from the west, and from the north and from the south, and shall sit down [lie at table] in the kingdom of God" (Luke 13:29). This chosen congregation of the kingdom will serve the Lord at the Messianic meal even in the kingdom of God. "Blessed are those servants whom the Lord when he comes shall find watching; verily, I say unto you that he shall gird himself and make them sit down to meat, and will come forth and serve them" (Luke 12:37). The Messianic meal may be likened to a wedding supper at which the Messiah-Son-of-Man weds his chosen congregation, the pure bride. This idea of a wedding also pervades the kingdom-of-God parables of Jesus: the bringer of the heavenly kingdom appears as the celestial bridegroom, the chosen of the kingdom of God are the invited guests, and the congregation itself is the bride.

Jesus' Last Supper

But this was not only a promise for the future. Jesus was convinced that this promise was already beginning to be fulfilled on earth in his own lifetime, that it was his mission to gather the members of the future kingdom into a fellowship; that in fact the kingdom of God had already appeared with his coming. For that reason, too, the fundamental mood of the fellowship that formed around him was one of nuptial rejoicing over the dawning of the promised Last Days. In speaking to the disciples of John the Baptist, Jesus explained why he did not favor fasting in the words: "Can the wedding guests mourn as long as the bridegroom is with them?" (Matt. 9:15).

The supper that Jesus shared with his disciples on the night of his betrayal must be understood wholly in terms of this anticipation of the kingdom of God. Knowing himself to be the Messiah who will be brought to his glory through persecution and death, Jesus unites himself with his disciples here on earth and sits down with them to partake of the Messianic repast. He initiates here on earth a fellowship of the table that extends over into the celestial kingdom.

"I shall not drink again of this fruit of the vine until that day when I drink it new with you in my Father's kingdom" (Matt. 26:29).

The Breaking of Bread,
and the Epiphanies of the Resurrected Christ

While this promise may have been discredited by the death of Jesus, it was overwhelmingly confirmed by the reappearances of the resurrected Christ, the first taking place on Easter morning. These appearances are closely connected with the implications of the Messianic meal and the perpetuation of the Messianic fellowship of the table; specifically, with a perpetuation of the breaking of bread as the Lord had done at his Last Supper. From the very beginning these two elements were linked. The accounts of the resurrection in the Gospels and in the Acts of the Apostles make it plain that many of the epiphanies of the resurrected Christ were related to the fellowship's breaking of bread.

The Christian community, therefore, saw these encounters with the resurrected Christ as the confirmation of all their ardent expectations of salvation. The kingdom of heaven had already begun in their midst; the new life had already emerged among them and was moving majestically toward its complete fulfillment. The heavenly wedding supper had begun; the bride (i.e., the Church, the congregation) was prepared for the bridegroom, and the seer, St. John, had already glimpsed the climax of the process of redemption. John heard the voice of a great multitude crying: "Hallelujah! For the Lord our God the Almighty reigns. Let us rejoice and exult and give him glory, for the marriage of the Lamb has come, and his Bride has made herself ready" (Rev. 19:6–7).

The Paschal Rejoicing

This rejoicing is the basic mood of the Church at the Eucharistic meal. The hearts of the partakers in the meal are filled with nuptial gladness. In Acts 2:46 we are told expressly: "And breaking bread in their homes, they partook of food with glad and generous hearts, praising God." The communion with the risen Lord gives rise to gladness, for the communicant experiences the presence of the Redeemer and is assured that he himself belongs to the kingdom of God. The celestial wedding supper had begun, the kingdom of God was come, blissful communion with the Lord already existed. The Orthodox liturgy has preserved unchanged this early Christian mood of rejoicing and spiritual gladness. In this its character is quite different from the Eucharist in, say, Reformed Christianity, where the early Christian spirit of gladness is clouded over and obscured by the spirit of penitence.

The mood of nuptial rejoicing is particularly well expressed in the hymns of the Orthodox Easter liturgy. The Easter canon of John of Damascus, sung on Easter Sunday, begins with the words: "So be it! Let us drink a New Drink, not a miraculous potion from parched rocks, but the spring of immortality that flows from the tomb of Christ, in which waters we come to power."

In accord with its mood of charismatic rejoicing, the early Church even permitted ritual dancing; later this was banned on grounds of propriety. It has, however, survived in the Ethiopian liturgy. The hymns of the Orthodox liturgy still mention the religious dance of rejoicing, which is derived from the dance of David before the Ark of the Covenant (2 Sam. 6:14). In the Easter canon of John of Damascus we find in the liturgy for Easter morning: "David, the ancestor in God, danced and leaped before the Ark of the Covenant. But we, God's holy people, behold the fulfillment of your signs. Let us then rejoice, inspired by God, for that Christ Omnipotent arose." There is also a reference to dance in the following Easter *stichera*[1]: "Cease your looking, ye women, ye bearers of the tidings of

---

[1] *stichos* (Gk.) = verse of a psalm; *sticheron* (plural: *stichera*) = liturgical strophe, originally sung to a *stichos*.

Salvation; tell unto Zion: Take from us the joyous tidings of Christ's Resurrection. Rejoice, dance in the ring and shout with jubilation, O Jerusalem, beholding Christ, the King: Like a bridegroom he steps forth from the grave."

The nuptial image occurs in another verse by John of Damascus: "Let us haste, bearing torches, toward Christ, who comes like a bridegroom from the tomb, and with the multitude of lovers of feasts let us celebrate God's redeeming Pascha."[2] The rejoicing becomes an ecstatic stammering, and the liturgy itself has retained the stammering jubilation of the earliest Christian community. "The holy Pascha is today shown to us. The new, holy Pascha. The mystic Pascha. The wholly revered Pascha. The Pascha, Christ, the Savior. The irreproachable Pascha. The great Pascha. The believers' Pascha. The Pascha that opens the gates of paradise to us. The Pascha that sanctifies all believers. . . . The Pascha of rejoicing. The Pascha of the Lord, the Pascha. The wholly revered Pascha was revealed to us. Pascha, in joy let us embrace one another. O Pascha, redeeming us from sorrow. For today Christ shone out of the grave as out of a chamber. The womenfolk filled He with joy when He said: Bear to the apostles the tidings."

This miracle—that in breaking bread with Christ in accordance with a ritual taught them by Jesus himself at the Messianic wedding supper the fellowship of the baptized are once again in the presence of the Redeemer—is the real creative core of the Orthodox liturgy. And the congregation feel it to be so, feel that they themselves are witnessing the epiphanies of the resurrected Christ.

Liturgical Productivity

This mystery has not only become the creative source for the spiritual life of the Orthodox Church; it has also given rise to an immeasurable wealth of liturgical forms, all of which further glorify the mystery. The body of liturgy that

[2] Pascha (Gk., from Heb.) = the Easter meal at which the Easter lamb was eaten.

grew up in the Eastern Church from the first to the sixth centuries constitutes one of the most magnificent creations of Christian piety. Judged solely in terms of their formal, stylistic and artistic qualities, the Eastern liturgies can be compared only with Greek tragedy. The conviction on the part of each congregation that in breaking bread in the Eucharist they were continuing that personal encounter with the risen Lord which had been vouchsafed to the apostles, unleashed a productivity that we find absolutely amazing. Here is the place to state the thesis, which we shall more fully develop later, that at the beginning of the history of the Church, variety rather than uniformity was the rule. This is particularly true for the development of the liturgy. We need only compare the simple form of the liturgy for the Eucharist as it is found in the *Teaching of the Twelve Apostles* (*Didache,* first century) with the liturgies of the fifth and sixth centuries in order to see what tremendous creative elaboration had been at work. It would be totally incorrect to say that these later elaborations are degenerate varieties of an originally uniform liturgy. On the contrary, the concept of the Eucharist and the subsequent mood of rejoicing and jubilation were in themselves so inspiring that they unleashed an almost uncontrollable impulse to create ever new and various forms of worship.

Coordination of the Liturgy
in the Byzantine Imperial Church

The older liturgies that have come down to us—above all, the *Didache,* the "Clementine" liturgy, the Syrian liturgy, the St. James' liturgy of the Church of Jerusalem, the Nestorian and Persian liturgies, the Egyptian liturgy that goes by the name of St. Mark's, the Euchologion of Serapion, the liturgy preserved in the Egyptian Church which probably goes back to Hippolytus—all these convey an impressive picture of variety. The coordination of liturgy took place only in conjunction with the extension and nationalization of the Byzantine Church. Finally, from the sixth

century on, two standard types of liturgy were established
under canon law. The first was the so-called liturgy of
St. John Chrysostom; it is patterned closely after the liturgy
traditionally employed in the city of Constantinople. Bearing the name of one of the most famous Ecumenical Patriarchs, this liturgy spread from *Hagia Sophia* throughout
the whole of the Byzantine Church, just as in the Carolingian Empire the liturgy employed in the Roman Mass was
established as the standard. This meant the extinction of the
numerous other liturgies that had been in use within the
far-flung sphere of the Byzantine Church, just as the Carolingian reform spelled the doom of the older Gallican,
Mozarabic and Celtic liturgies, which, incidentally, bore a
close resemblance to Eastern liturgy.

Alongside the Chrysostom liturgy, St. Basil's liturgy also
survived, thanks to the enormous prestige and power of
monasticism in the Orthodox Church. St. Basil's liturgy—
which probably was created by that famous Church Father
—was originally the liturgy of the Cappadocian monasteries.
It could scarcely be banished from the Byzantine monasteries, but it is celebrated only ten times a year. In addition
to these two liturgies there is a third called the "Liturgy
of the Presanctified Elements." It is ascribed to Pope Gregory the Great. This liturgy is unique in that the consecration
of the Eucharistic elements is absent from it; communion
does indeed take place, after the verbal part of the service
is spoken, but the necessary Eucharistic elements have been
consecrated on the preceding Sunday. This liturgy is celebrated mornings on the weekdays of Lent and from Monday to Wednesday of Easter week.

This hoard of richly varied liturgies testifies to the existence of an enormous creative freedom during the early centuries of the Christian era. This freedom must have been
accompanied by a religious élan, a capacity for liturgical
improvisation, such as no longer exists and such as we find
difficult even to imagine. This does not mean that the liturgy
was the product of arbitrary individual decisions. Rather,

it drew upon already existing liturgies from various sources, combining and modifying these into new forms that expressed the charismatic impulses of the Church.

Variety within the Liturgy

The proclaiming of a specific, official standard for the entire Orthodox Church did not mean a "freezing" of the liturgy. The impulse toward variations in the divine services could find expression in the most multifarious ways. In the Eastern Orthodox Church, as in the Roman Mass and the Roman Breviary, a distinction is made between "fixed" and "alternating" parts. While the fixed parts of the order of divine worship are unalterable and form the basic structure of any given service, the individual character of the service or the particular Church feast can be given its due in the movable parts. These parts consist of readings from the Old and New Testaments which are relevant to the special nature of the given feast and of prayers and hymns. They constitute one of the spiritual treasures of the Eastern Orthodox Church; for the Church is rich in the possession of hymns by her greatest holy men and inspired saints. These are incorporated into the very liturgy of the Church and thus are kept alive by the body of believers.

All aspects of the liturgy show this fundamental variety.

The Liturgical Gestures

The Orthodox Church can draw upon a great wealth of liturgical gestures. In most Protestant churches it is customary for worshipers to sit on chairs or benches while sending their prayers up to God. This practice is unknown in the Orthodox Church and would be incomprehensible to the Orthodox believer. For he takes part in services standing and prays standing, with his arms at his sides, except when he crosses himself at the beginning and end of the prayer. The commandment to stand is explicitly stated in the liturgy: Before the reading of the Gospel the priest, standing at the royal gate of the sanctuary, cries out, "Wisdom! Let us stand erect!" Clasping hands in prayer is unknown to the Orthodox Church. This gesture derives from an ancient Germanic tradition; it symbolizes the prisoning of the sword hand by the left hand—in other words, making oneself defenseless and delivering up oneself to the protection of God. The Roman Catholic gesture of palms pressed together, fingertips pointing upward, symbolizes the flame; it too is unknown in the Orthodox Church. However, the gamut of gestures in use in the Eastern Church is great: crossing; bowing with arms dangling; kneeling; touching the floor with the hand; prostration on the floor, arms outstretched, forehead pressed against the floor. As a penitential gesture there is the crossing of arms and pounding on the chest. The liturgists pray standing, sometimes with arms outstretched in the form of a cross, sometimes crossed over the chest. Even the gesture of prayer used in antiquity—both arms held up, palms turned upward—is employed for certain passages of the liturgy, for example, for the eulogy of the cherubim and for invoking the descent of the Holy Spirit upon the Eucharistic elements. In addition there are many other gestures of worship and adoration: kissing the holy icons, kissing the altar, the Gospels, the crucifix with which the priest dispenses the concluding blessing, kissing the hem of the priest's robe.

The Liturgical Vestments

Great variety is also exhibited in the liturgical vestments, whose embellishment has become a highly developed branch of sacred art. These robes have a symbolic significance which is set forth in the preface to the Eucharistic liturgy, the *proskomide*. Before beginning the service of the Eucharist, priests and deacons don the holy vestments in the sanctuary behind the iconostasis. As they do so they speak certain prayers that proclaim the spiritual meaning of their act. Donning the ecclesiastical robes is a symbol for donning a new spiritual nature, the assumption of a celestial body. In putting on these spiritual garments the celebrant is the representative of paradisial man as he will achieve restitution and perfection in the kingdom of God. As he dons the long, smooth undergarment, the *sticharion,* which corresponds approximately to the Roman alb, the priest pronounces the following prayer: "My soul rejoices in the Lord; He has dressed me in the garment of salvation and put upon me the vestment of joy. Like a bridegroom He has placed the miter upon me, and like a bride He has surrounded me with adornment." The note of nuptial rejoicing is sounded even in these preparations for the Eucharist: in changing his dress and putting on his new nature, the priest becomes bridegroom and bride.

The next article of dress, the *epitrachelion,* corresponds to the Roman stole. It is worn by the Orthodox priest around his neck, and the dangling ends are sewed together over his chest. It signifies the outpouring of the Holy Spirit. In putting on this garment the priest says: "Praise be to God who has poured out His grace upon His priests like precious ointment upon the head; it flows down upon the beard, yea, upon the beard of Aaron; it flows down upon the hem of his garment." In donning the girdle the priest prays to God: "He who has girded me with strength and made my way irreproachable." Similarly, in putting on the *epimanikia*—cuffs reaching from wrist to elbow, somewhat resembling the Roman maniple—the priest says as he places it on his right arm: "Thy right arm was glorified in strength, O Lord; Thy right arm, O Lord, shattered the enemy"; and for his left arm: "Thy hands have created me and formed me; teach me, that I may know Thy commandments." The donning of the *phelonion* [chasuble], which like the Lord's tunic is seamless (John 19:23) and whose color conforms to the calendar feast to be celebrated, is compared with the "clothing of the priests in righteousness" (Ps. 132:9).

Liturgical Symbolism: "Promise" and "Fulfillment"

It is not easy for the non-Orthodox to understand the language of the Orthodox liturgy, for a special mode of thought underlies the texts and hymns—a way of thinking primarily in symbols and not in abstract concepts. This very fact gives a singular unity to liturgy, meditation and prayer. The majority of the images that serve as signs and symbols of particular spiritual processes are derived from the immeasurably rich pictorial world of the Old and New Testaments. They are, therefore, already sacral images. But these images are not beheld in terms of their literal, superficial pictorial values; they are linked to one another in a special "mystical" fashion. The basic underlying idea is that the Old and New Testaments stand in a mysterious relation of "promise" and "fulfillment" to one another. The Old Testament represents the era of the promise; in it the great mysteries of the New Testament—the era of fulfillment—are prefigured in prophetic signs and symbols. Thus the Old and New Testaments are interwoven in a pattern of redemptory correspondences.

Early examples of this thinking in terms of correspondences can already be found in the arguments of the Apostle Paul—when, for example, he interprets the cloud in the desert as a foreshadowing of the mystery of baptism, or when he sees the rock that moved through the desert giving water to the people of Israel as the symbol of Christ (1 Cor. 10:1 ff.). In the Alexandrian school of catechumens, this typological, anagogic interpretation of the Old and New Testaments was set up as a regular method of scholarship and theology. The mode of thinking operating in this linking of symbols springs directly from the kind of typological exegesis taught by Clement of Alexandria and Origen.

A simple example will cast light on the nature of this figurative thinking. During the first week of Lent the prayers and hymns in the liturgy deal with the theme of fasting. Fasting itself is described in sheer imagery. The *triodion* of Theodore of Studion which belongs in the liturgy for Monday morning of the first week of Lent, goes as follows: "Now it is come, the true time of the struggles for victory has begun. Let us joyfully begin with fasting the racetrack of the fasts, carrying virtues as gifts before the Lord." Here the thought is couched in terms of the images of racing and competition, favorite images of the Apostle Paul's. Monday of the first week of Lent is the beginning of the contest in which the Christian drives his chariot on to the racetrack of fasting in order to strive for the victory of holiness.

Another device is the use of typological images. In another ode by Theodore of Studion we find: "Purified by fasting on Mount Horeb, Elijah saw God. We too wish to purify our hearts by fasting. Thus we shall see Christ." Here the prophet Elijah is invoked, who, as the prototype of the ascetic of the desert, is the Old Testament sponsor of fasting.

In another ode by the same hymnist, fasting is again traced to sacred prototypes: "By the measure of his forty-day fast the Lord consecrated and hallowed the present days, O brethren. In these days, then, let us cry out eagerly: Christ praises and raises into the eons." Here Christ himself, he who has fulfilled the redemption, appears as the archetype of fasting. His forty-day fast in the desert serves as an example for all his disciples; from it springs the whole principle of ecclesiastical fasting, which has been set up as a general Christian road to sanctity. This same type of figurative thinking underlies the liturgical texts of all the mysteries; in each case they are related to and justified by archetypes from the Old and New Testaments.

2. THE SACRAMENTS

Nature and Number of the Sacraments

The mystery of Christ is announced and unfolded in the Church through an abundance of sacraments and sacramentals. The Roman Church has its seven sacraments, but the Eastern Church sets no such limits. Under the influence of Roman Catholicism, it is true, the Orthodox theologians adopted the concept of the seven sacraments; but this means little, since Orthodoxy does not make any strict distinction between sacraments and sacramentals, the latter being ecclesiastical rituals that are not sacraments in the narrow sense of the word. A sacrament is, to quote the definition in the catechism drawn up by Metropolitan Filaret of Moscow, "a holy act by which grace, or what is the same thing, the redeeming power of God, operates upon man in mysterious fashion." At bottom all rites of the Church are outflowings of the original mystery of Christ and perpetuate the incarnation of Christ and its redemptory effect through the ages.

The New Testament records a number of such "holy acts," not all of which have been accepted as sacraments of the Church. For example, baptism and the Eucharist have become established sacraments, while the washing of feet, which in the Gospel of John appears in place of the Lord's Supper, has not been so adopted, probably for reasons of propriety. Still, certain metropolitan churches and certain monasteries have retained this washing of feet as a special ritual; usually the abbot washes the feet of twelve brothers, or the bishop those of twelve poor men.

In a certain sense the whole sphere of the Church is *mysteriogen,* that is to say, out of its charismatic plenitude it can go on creating new mysteries forever. The primitive Church had established the definitive canon of the New Testament by the fourth century. The fixed forms of dogma were worked out in the period between the fifth to the seventh century. Liturgy was coordinated in the seventh century. But by the end of the first millennium, the number of sacraments was not yet fixed. This is an indication of the creative vitality in that particular realm.

Dionysius the Pseudo-Areopagite, one of the great doctors of the Orthodox Church, cites six mysteries in his book *On the Ecclesiastical Hierarchy:* baptism, Eucharist, *myron* unction, ordination, tonsure, and the rites for the dead. Two hundred years later John of Damascus speaks of only two sacraments: baptism with accompanying confirmation, and the Eucharist. The Greek theologians did not accept the number of seven sacraments until the Council of Lyon (1274), in the course of the negotiations for union with Rome; these sacraments had been established by Western scholastic theology only a short time before: baptism, confirmation, Eucharist, penance, ordination, marriage, unction for the sick.

There are many in the ranks of present-day Orthodox theologians who do not abide by any rigid limitation of the mysteries to the seven sacraments approved by the Roman Catholic Church. These theologians point out that the Orthodox Church shows far more latitude in its attitude toward the mysteries. Moreover, the most important rituals of the Eastern Church represent a group of "holy acts," and incorporate procedures bearing on several mysteries. The sacrament of baptism is a good example. This consists not only of threefold immersion of the candidate; preceding it is a threefold renunciation of Satan, the candidate standing first with his face to the west, the direction of the Antichrist, and spitting at Satan three times, then turning to the east and surrendering himself to his new Lord, Christ. Immediately after baptism proper comes the *myron* unction (anointing with consecrated oil). Just as after the baptism in the Jordan the Holy Spirit descended upon Jesus in the form of a dove, so the baptism is capped by the believer's receiving the "seal of the gift of the Holy Ghost," as it is called in the liturgy. Cyril of Jerusalem explained this mystery in his third mystagogic catechism in the following fashion: "After you have been deemed worthy of this holy act of anointment, you are called Christians (*christos* = the Anointed). . . . For before you were deemed worthy of this grace, you were not really worthy of this name of Christian, but were only, as it were, on the way to it." In

the West the immediate sequence of baptism and anointment was broken up; in Roman Catholicism today confirmation takes place only after "first communion."

The Eucharist as a Mystery Play

The entire complex of mysteries of the Orthodox Church
revolves around the prime mystery: the death and resurrection of Christ.

Since it stands at the heart of all the mysteries of the
Church, the Eucharistic liturgy can be properly understood
only within the organism of the other mysteries. We can,
therefore, hope to offer only a brief introduction to the
mystery of the Eucharist. A word of warning: it is important not to make any hasty identification of the Eucharist
with the Roman Mass. The present-day Roman Mass represents a later stage of liturgical development. Basic elements of the liturgy of the early Church have been dropped,
above all the separation between a special service for
catechumens and the Eucharist for believers. The procedure of the Roman Mass is therefore simpler than the procedure of the Eucharist. Spiritually and theologically, too,
it proceeds from a different conception of the nature of the
sacrament.

Jewish and Greek forms of worship found their way into
the liturgy of the Eastern Church. The traditions of the late
Jewish synagogue worship were merged with ritual practices of Hellenistic mystery religions—both reinterpreted in
a characteristically Christian sense. The basic character of
the Eucharistic liturgy, however, owes more to the Hellenistic element. The Eucharist in its present Orthodox form
differs very little from the Eucharistic celebration used in
the primitive Church. It is an elaborate, complicated
mystery play.

The liturgy, first of all, is divided into two parts, one
for the catechumens and one for the believers. This feature
is a survival from a time when the Church was still a missionary Church and was filling its ranks mostly with adults

who had first to be instructed in Christian doctrine as catechumens. Only after this were they inducted into the Christian mysteries and entitled to participate in the first part of the services. They were still excluded from the central mystery of the Eucharist because they had not yet undergone baptism. During this period of preparation the catechumens were admitted only to that part of the Eucharistic service which consisted mainly of sermon and prayer. They had to leave after the sermon, when the time came for the enactment of the Eucharistic mystery itself.

It was therefore assumed that the congregation contained a large number of the as yet unbaptized adult catechumens. The architecture of the early churches took account of this, for the end of the nave was partitioned off as a special, separated anteroom for the catechumens. As a preliminary to full membership in the Church the former pagan was introduced into the anteroom of the church and allowed to attend the first part of the mystery service. Accordingly the first part of the Eucharistic liturgy ends with a thrice repeated cry: "Ye catechumens, go out. No catechumens!"

Then the initiates, the baptized believers, are left among themselves, and the Eucharist begins. Again and again, stress is laid upon its peculiar nature as a mystery. Before the singing of the Creed, the priest calls out: "The doors, the doors!" Originally these words were directed to the doorkeepers who were required to close the doors before recitation of the Creed, so that no uninitiate could hear. That is to say, the Creed was regarded as a secret formula, not to be taught to the catechumens until just before their baptism. The mystery is again stressed in the call, "Holiness to the holy!" which the priest addresses to the congregation just before breaking the bread, as a last warning to receive the mystery worthily. There is also this passage in the communion prayer: "As partaker in Thy mysterious communion take me up today, O Son of God, for I will not betray Thy secret to Thine enemies, nor give Thee a kiss like that of Judas." Before receiving communion the believer renews his vow not to betray the mystery to God's enemies. Although the congregation is no longer broken up into a large group of adult catechumens and a presumably smaller group of baptized believers, the Orthodox Church still follows all the procedures that arose out of this missionary situation.

The Divine Presence

There is another striking difference between the Orthodox Eucharist and the Roman Mass. The Roman Mass reaches its climax, both in structure and in theological significance, when, at the recitation of the prescribed words by the priest, the elements of the bread and the wine become the Body and Blood of Christ. These two moments are dramatized to the congregation by the ringing of the sacring bell and the elevation and adoration of the transformed elements.

The Eucharistic liturgy of the Orthodox Church follows quite another pattern. No bell is rung at any time to announce the climax of the ceremony. The whole ritual is a mystery drama reenacting the entire history of redemption, the incarnation, death and resurrection of the Logos, and the outpouring of the Holy Spirit. The Orthodox Church too lays great stress upon the fact that in the course of the mystery an actual transformation of the Eucharistic elements of bread and wine takes place. And under the influence of the Roman Catholic dogma of transubstantiation a kind of doctrine of transubstantiation has been developed, for the Orthodox Church also felt the impact of the doctrinal disputes of the Reformation age. But the transformation of the elements themselves is not the central issue for the Orthodox believer. For him the central event of the Eucharist is the descent, the appearance, the divine presence of the resurrected Christ. And the full import of this event colors every moment of the liturgy. The believer's partaking of Communion, and his attitude toward the mystery of the Communion, are governed by the thought that he is actually encountering the living person of the Lord who enters the congregation as "King of the universe borne invisibly over their spears by the angelic hosts."

The congregation is, in fact, frequently reminded of this matter. After the great Eucharistic prayer, the priest cries: "Christ is in the midst of us!" And the assisting priest answers, after receiving the kiss of peace: "He is with us and will be." This cry is repeated in the same form immediately after the priests' communion. The assertion is made again while the Communion is being dispensed, for the choir bursts out in highly dramatic fashion with the chant: "Blessed is he who comes in the name of the Lord. God is the Lord and has appeared to us." And after the distribution the choir sings:

> "We have seen the true light;
> We have received the Holy Spirit;
> We have found the true faith.
> Let us worship the inseparable Trinity,
>   for it has redeemed us."

The personal presence of Christ brings about the transformation of the elements. Since this is so, preservation and display of the consecrated Host after the Eucharistic liturgy is unknown in the Orthodox Church. The Messianic meal is so completely bound up with the immediate presence of the resurrected Lord that the consecrated elements actualize their mystical content only during the Eucharist itself; at any other time adoration of the elements is impossible. This alone shows how far apart this dynamic, spiritual, personalized conception of the Eucharist is from the Roman doctrine of transubstantiation. In the Orthodox ritual the transformation does not take place during the recitation of the introductory words. Rather, there follows an additional liturgical act, the *epiklesis,* in which priest and deacon stand before the altar with arms outspread and hands raised, imploring the Holy Spirit to descend upon the Eucharistic elements. Immediately thereafter the deacon fans the "air" above the elements, using a special liturgical cloth for the purpose. In this way he represents the movement of the descending Holy Spirit. In some versions of the liturgy the *epiklesis* includes the words "transubstantiating by Thy Holy Spirit," but there is no such phrase in the liturgy of St. Basil.

By the same token the character of the Eucharist as a sacrifice is not so strongly emphasized in the Orthodox Church as it is in the Roman Mass and the Roman doctrine of the sacraments. To be sure, the Eucharist represents the bloodless sacrifice wherein the sacrifice of Christ on the cross is repeated in mystical fashion, but this idea is overshadowed by the larger concept of the Eucharist as a mystery presenting the whole story of redemption, the incarnation of the divine Logos as well as his suffering, death and resurrection. To the mind of the Orthodox believer, the real significance of the Eucharist lies not so much in the repetition of the sacrifice of Golgotha, but in the encounter with the living, resurrected Lord.

Eucharist and Congregation

Just as veneration of the Eucharistic elements is not separated from the Eucharistic liturgy, so also consecration is not performed without a congregation. Celebration of the Eucharist by a priest without a congregation present is unthinkable in an Orthodox church. The congregation plays a vital part in the Eucharistic liturgy. It makes the mystery possible. It is invited to the meal and takes part in it. Christ comes down into its midst. The meaning of the mystery is the union of the earthly and the celestial congregations brought about by the descent of the resurrected Christ. This is why the priest elevates the Eucharistic elements and cries out: "We bring Thee what is Thine from those who are Thine, to all and for all." Since the Orthodox Church has always adhered to this fundamental interpretation, its ritual never underwent that degeneration which overcame the

Mass during the Middle Ages and which called forth the wrath of the Reformers.

Correspondingly the Orthodox Church has also adhered to the original form of communion "under both kinds," that is, partaking of the Bread and the Wine. The Latin manner of dispensing the sacrament seems to the Orthodox believer a violation of the form of the Eucharist as it was instituted by Christ himself. It seems to him also a sin against brotherly love, since the priest is elevated above the layman by receiving preferential treatment in the partaking of the Wine. The Orthodox Church generously admits even small children to communion after their baptism and chrismation, thus making them table companions of the resurrected Lord.

III.

Dogma

1. GENERAL REMARKS

Orthodox Dogma and the Greek Spirit

Adolf von Harnack, the celebrated Protestant historian of the Church, decided that dogma was a product of "Hellenization of Christianity on a grand scale." By this he meant that the original message of Jesus and the apostles had been reinterpreted in the light of Greek philosophy. On the whole his attitude toward dogma was a negative one. That is to say, he regarded it as an aspect of the degeneration in Christianity. Transforming the gospel into doctrine was, to his mind, an intellectualistic distortion. Furthermore, he held that the spirit of Greek philosophy had introduced foreign, unevangelical elements into the religion.

There is no doubt that such "hellenization" actually took place. We need only look at the creeds of the ecumenical councils of the early Church to see this. Elements of the Neoplatonic metaphysics of substance and the doctrine of hypostasis certainly went into the formulation of the Church's doctrine of the Trinity, into its Christology and into its anthropology. But should this phenomenon properly be termed degeneracy?

Undoubtedly Harnack was committed to the Protestant idea that the Church should rest upon "pure doctrine." The Orthodox theologian takes quite a different view of dogma. He too would not deny the impress made by the Greek spirit upon the development of dogma. On the contrary, he tends to emphasize and extol it. He holds that the formation of the dogma was not a purely human process, whereas Harnack considered it to be an inevitable falsification of divine truths because of the inadequacy of human concepts. The Orthodox theologian sees the formation of dogma as a divine and human process modeled upon the incarnation of the divine Logos in the man Jesus Christ. The Holy Spirit, proceeding from God, intervened in the history of human thought. Consequently the dogma has two aspects. In one respect its truths, having their origin in divine revelation, are divine, eternal, unassailable and immutable. In the historical respect, however, the human mind is continuously striving to achieve a deeper understanding and a closer grasp of these truths. The eternal and immutable nature of dogma derives from its source in divine revelation, but the human grasp of it is subject to historical progression. Man can never understand the transcendental abstractly; he can know it only in its concrete embodiment in language. The hellenization of Christianity, therefore, was a historical process; it was natural that dogmatic truth should be apprehended in the spirit of Greek thought, since this was the dominant mode of thought during the era of the early Church.

Dogma as the Expression of the Mind of the Church

This conception of dogma is in keeping with the nature of belief itself. All genuine faith is ultimately founded upon direct transcendental experience. But genuine faith is also impelled to clarify intellectually its underlying ideas. The dogma of the Church, however, represents not the expression of an individual mind, but the expression of the mind of the Church as a whole meditating upon the facts of redemption; not the experience of isolated individuals, but the experience of the Church in its totality as a divine and human organism.

Dogma and Liturgy

Harnack's thesis is faulty in other respects. He does not understand that Orthodox dogma does not occupy the same isolated position within the Church as do doctrine and creed in the Protestant churches. Rather, dogma is part and parcel of the liturgical life of the Church. The creeds of the Orthodox Church are not abstract formulations of a "pure doctrine." They are hymns of adoration which have their place in the liturgy. There is a statement of dogma in the baptismal creed that the proselyte speaks in praise of God and in proclamation of the divine truth of salvation. Similarly, in the Eucharistic liturgy God is adored in the words of the credo before the priest invokes the descent of the Holy Spirit upon the Eucharistic elements. Thus dogma has fully preserved its original liturgical function in the Orthodox Church.

Moreover, in the view of the Orthodox Church the liturgy is the proper place for dogma, not theological summas and textbooks. This is particularly true for the Eucharistic liturgy, this liturgy being a mystical unfolding of the full abundance of divine acts of redemption and divinely revealed truths. Liturgy and dogma, worship and creed, prayer and theological meditation and speculation are therefore inseparable. The dogma is a component of the living worship. Intellectual definition of the truths of the Christian faith is necessary, of course, and certainly that is one of the functions of dogma. But in the Orthodox Church dogma is not limited to differentiating Christian principles from "false doctrines." It governs the Christian's religious and moral life; that is, it has a practical side. It promotes growth in the Christian's spiritual life by keeping the facts of redemption ever present in his mind.

2. ORTHODOX AND ROMAN CATHOLIC
IDEAS OF DOGMA

Because dogma has this practical function within the spiritual organism of the Orthodox Church, it has not undergone so much theoretical elaboration as the dogma of Roman Catholicism or Protestantism. The various elements of the Creed have not been defined with precision. Hence there is much greater freedom in the interpretation of the dogma. Even the formulation of a dogma by an ecumenical council is not *eo ipso* necessarily binding under canon law. To be binding, a dogma must also be accepted by the general consensus of the Church, what the theologians call the "ecumenical conscience."

It is obvious from all this that the development and content of Orthodox dogma cannot be simply equated with analogous phenomena in the Roman Catholic Church. Comparisons with Roman Catholic and Protestant ideas can, however, be illuminating. By studying certain parallel tenets we can more readily understand the special character of Orthodox belief.

Occidental Christianity

[a] RELIGION AS A LEGAL RELATIONSHIP. From the beginning the West has understood the fundamental relationship between God and man primarily as a *legal* relationship. This emerges, for example, in the interpretation of redemption given by St. Paul in his Epistle to the Romans. Paul's approach reflects the fact that in Rome he was dealing with a largely Jewish-Christian congregation whose members knew the Law. They were men fervently concerned with the question of God's justice and men's obligation to meet the demands of a just God. This legalistic way of thinking, which so dominated the Judeo-Christian groups in the Roman community, was quite in harmony with the fundamental Roman attitude toward religion. To

the pagan Romans, too, the relationship between the gods and man was primarily legalistic. For the pagan Roman the political aspect of this legalistic relationship remained in the foreground; in Rome, worship was state worship, the priest functioned as a government official and combined his office with high posts in the state, and the main emphasis of the religion was upon the public weal. The legalistic character of the religion was further manifested in the strict regulation of all ceremonies of public worship. Words, gestures, clothing, rites, time and place—all were prescribed in detail. In attention to minutiae the pagan Romans were no whit less exacting than the Jews. When, therefore, Paul repeatedly spoke of "justification before the law," he was in fact being a Roman unto the Romans.

[b] THE LEGALISTIC ATTITUDE OF THE CHURCH. Roman Catholicism continued to develop in this direction. Rome elaborated the specifically Western view of the sacrament of penance which depends completely on the idea of "justification." God has established certain laws for man. By sinful conduct man violates these laws. Justice requires him to make amends to God. The Church supervises this legal relationship. The bishop is the agent of the Church; he determines the degree of sinfulness and decides in which cases and under what conditions penance is possible. The priest, a subagent of the Church ordained by the bishop, also decides what payment the sinner owes to God. Just as jurisprudence has drawn up scales of crime and punishment, so also the Church has drawn up a scale of sins and the necessary penances. The business of the Church's "legal agents" is to apply this scale to particular cases.

Latent in this legalistic view of the sacrament of penance were the potentialities for subsequent degeneration of the sacrament—as, for example, the idea of the indulgence. The indulgence sprang from a merging of Roman and Germanic legal ideas; its basis is the assumption that penances can be reduced, and above all that amends can be made by contributions of money. Once the principle was established, the ecclesiastical authorities could set up a fixed tariff; a given amount of money could be substituted for a given act of penance.

The same legalism also governed the development of the concept of the Church and the role of the priesthood. The Church regards itself as a spiritual legal institution which Christ founded by virtue of divine law. The priest is the legitimate representative of divine law and order. Only within the framework of such legalistic thinking could the papacy and the idea of papal primacy have come into existence. In the Roman Church the political ideas of antiquity and Catholic legal thinking merged to create a new form. This new form was able to arise in the political vacuum of the period of the great migrations, in a Rome no longer dominated by an emperor. Under the political conditions of the Middle Ages the Roman bishop acquired by default many of the legal and political functions that had hitherto belonged to the imperial power. His claim was that Christ himself had founded the papacy when he transferred his spiritual powers to Peter. As papal doctrine was developed, the idea of jurisdictional supremacy played a major part in it. The popes added the powers of a sovereign to those they already possessed as priests, and donned the imperial crown in addition to the episcopal tiara. At the height of this development a Pope would proclaim himself supreme ruler of the world. He would have it that Christ had handed him the two swords of spiritual and secular power, and would regard kings and emperors as his feudal vassals on whom he conferred crown and scepter by his right as successor of Peter.

The individual priest's conception of his own office again reflects this legalistic idea. Ordination by the bishop gives the priest the legal right to administer the sacraments and to hold the "power of the keys." When the priest says to a sinner after confession, *"Ego te absolvo"* (*I* absolve you), he is exercising this judicial right.

This legalistic outlook led the Western Church to develop

its own canon law far more consistently and more exhaustively than the Eastern Church. From the very beginning Western canon law showed a tendency to extend its jurisdiction over everything in public or private life that had anything whatsoever to do with the Church. Thus canon law in the West penetrated, and indeed dominated, the whole life of society much more thoroughly than was the case in the realm of the Orthodox Church. Moreover, the creation of the autonomous Papal States was based upon the legalistic mentality. The Eastern Church did not aspire to such political independence.

[c] LEGALISTIC THINKING IN THEOLOGY. The legalistic way of thinking took root early in the theology of the Occident. While Paul's doctrine of justification never had any decisive importance in the East, we have indicated that it had far-flung consequences for the West. Continuing the tradition of Paul, Tertullian introduced a number of fundamental juristic concepts into theology. Then Augustine (354–430) made the doctrine of justification the basis of his conception of man's relation to God, and of his view of sin, guilt and grace. Anselm of Canterbury (1033–1109) viewed the legal relationship existing between God and man as the very cornerstone of all theological thinking, so much so that he believed he could logically deduce the truth of the Christian religion and the necessity for the incarnation of God from the idea of "satisfaction."[1] The covenantal theology of scholasticism regarded the history of salvation in general as a history of ever-renewed legal covenants between God and man.

This legalistic mentality also put its special stamp upon Western monasticism, which tended to stress "good works" and "supererogatory works"—the latter being works that the saintly man performs over and above those required to balance out his own sins. The concept of sanctity itself was

[1] Satisfaction is the doctrine that the sufferings and death of Christ satisfied the requirements of God's justice.

reshaped by this legalistic thinking. Alexander of Hales (†1245) went so far as to assert that through the satisfactions offered by Christ, the saints and the martyrs, a "hoard of good works" had been accumulated. This hoard, he said, was at the disposal of the Pope, who could use it for the benefit of believers in general.

Legalism even found its way into eschatology. In fact, when we examine Western notions of the "Last Days" we frequently have the impression that the idea of justice has completely triumphed over the idea of love. When that time comes mankind is to be strictly divided into a group of the saved, who will enter eternal bliss, and a group of the damned, who are condemned to eternal punishment. This doctrine of eternal damnation has always met with intense resistance in the East. Similarly the Eastern Church has never accepted the concept of purgatory that is so integral a part of the Roman Catholic scheme of salvation. By positing an intermediary state between heaven and hell, the Church allows the sinner another chance to improve his score before he must appear at the Last Judgment. The Church asserts its jurisdictional authority over this domain as well. By indulgences, Masses for the dead, and so on, it exercises its powers of binding and loosing over the souls in purgatory.

The idea of predestination, too, was taken up by the West and given a strong juridical cast. St. Augustine taught that the kingdom of God consisted of a fixed group of the elect, their number decreed by God from the beginning and corresponding to the number of the fallen angels. The purpose of history, he contended, was to separate the elect from the great masses of humanity. Only the elect are born to be citizens of the City of God. The legal standards governing the kingdom of God were fixed before all time by the inscrutable will of God. Redemption is founded upon a divine system of jurisprudence; man lives under its laws and on Judgment Day will be judged by its principles.

Orthodox Christianity

[a] BASIC MYSTICISM. The theology of the Eastern Church has quite another complexion. The differences may not be too precisely defined, since to do so would involve us in a series of generalities to which there will be numerous exceptions. We may, however, say that the striking feature of Eastern Christianity is its lack of those very features that depend on a conception of religion as a legal relationship. Instead, the mystical aspect of the New Testament message comes far more strongly to the fore. Both Pauline and Johannine mysticism are given equal weight. There is little emphasis upon justification. Instead, the major themes of the Orthodox faith are the apotheosis, sanctification, rebirth, re-creation, resurrection and transfiguration of man; and not only man, but also the whole universe—for the Eastern Church has a characteristically cosmic approach. The central theme is not God's justice but his love. For this reason the total development of religious life both within the Church and within the consciousness of each individual believer has taken a course radically different from that of the Western Church.

This matter is particularly striking when we consider the sacrament of penance. In the Eastern Church, penance is not associated with the idea of justification but with the idea of the Christian's education to a life of sanctity. Penance was never conceived of in legal terms, with the result that the sacrament never became corrupted. No doctrine or practice of indulgences ever arose. Since penance was always viewed as a road to sanctity rather than as an act of compensation, there could be no thought of substituting money payments for performance of acts of atonement.

Similarly, in the absence of a judicial conception, the Western doctrine of purgatory and of posthumous salvation by acts of the Church could not spread through the Eastern Orthodox Church. The Eastern Church never pretended that its powers to bind and loosen extended to the realm of the dead. The Eastern Church considered that its only power to affect the dead lay in intercessory prayer. Underlying this was the premise that the union between believers and the Body of Christ of which they are a part is not destroyed by death. This union continues to exist within the Church. This mystical communion in the Body of Christ makes possible a continuation of intercession and of vicarious suffering. Under these circumstances the institution of the Mass for the Dead also retained its purity and escaped the degeneration that took place in the West.

[b] THE MYSTICAL INTERPRETATION OF THE CHURCH. The Orthodox view of the nature of the Church is likewise not based upon any legalistic system. To be sure, a legal element does enter into its conception of ecclesiastical office, above all of the office of the bishop and of apostolic succession. But the legalistic idea is nowhere dominant; it is simply embedded in the view of the Church as the Mystical Body of Christ, and of the Holy Spirit as the continuous stream of life within the Church. There was no room in the Eastern faith for the idea of a Church-state, or for a bishop's exceeding his spiritual prerogatives and intervening in secular affairs. Consequently, the Eastern Church remained unaffected by the rise of the feudalistic state. Conditions that were characteristic of the Christian Middle Ages in the West, where bishops turned into the feudal lords of their dioceses, the dioceses themselves becoming territories and the bishops neglecting the spiritual side of their offices in favor of their political duties and their recreations as members of the feudal aristocracy, were totally unknown in the East. The bishops of the Eastern Orthodox Church have always remained first and foremost ecclesiastical officials. Many Orthodox bishops, it is true, felt it necessary to oppose godless princes, to admonish them in the name of Christ, and to call upon them to do penance. But these bishops never felt that their spiritual powers entitled them to claim secular dominion, or to treat secular rulers as feudal vassals of the Church.

The legalistic principle is likewise absent from the way
the ordinary Orthodox priest regards the nature of his
priesthood. Nowhere in the Orthodox liturgy does the priest
allude to his rightful title. Instead he repeatedly expresses
his own sinfulness and unworthiness, emphasizing that he is
no less a sinner than his parishioners. It is significant that
in the Orthodox sacrament of penance the formula of ab-
solution is not framed in declaratory terms. Instead of the
Roman priest's *"Ego te absolvo,"* the Orthodox priest says
after confession: "My spiritual child, you have now confessed to my lowliness. I, miserable sinner, do not have the
power to absolve a sin upon earth; only God can do that.
But for the sake of those divine words which were spoken
to the apostles after His resurrection, and which were: 'If
you forgive the sins of any, they are forgiven; if you retain
the sins of any, they are retained,' for the sake of those
words and trusting in them, we say this: 'What you have
confessed to my extreme lowliness, and also those things
which you did not say, either from ignorance or from for-
getfulness, whatever they are: may God forgive you for
them in this world and the next.' "

In the matter of sanctity, the Eastern Church venerates
the saints as spiritually gifted persons who have succeeded
in living on earth the "angelic" life of the celestial Church.
But their achievements are nowhere booked to the accounts
of the Church as "supererogatory works," nor has the
Church ever claimed a legal right from God to invest this
"capital."

[c] APOTHEOSIS. The great theme of Orthodox theology
has remained the incarnation of God and the apotheosis
of man. Always the emphasis has been upon rebirth, the
re-creation of man, his reshaping into a new creature, his
being resurrected along with Christ and rising with Christ
to God. Fulfillment of man's being and his transfiguration
by grace are all-important to the Orthodox theologian. It
is no wonder that the doctrine of justification has been given
short shrift in Orthodox dogmatics. The most famous ex-

position of Orthodox dogma, that of John of Damascus (c. 700–50), does not even mention the idea of justification. So the Orthodox Church was never prompted to assert that the necessity for God's incarnation arose logically out of the doctrine of satisfaction: the very groundwork for such a doctrine was lacking. Not until Protestant ideas penetrated the East during the sixteenth and seventeenth centuries were the Orthodox theologians compelled to take a position on the doctrine of justification. The result was a "pseudomorphosis" of the whole of Orthodox theology. That is to say, a violent wrench was given to the entire theology.

The basic Orthodox attitude is again reflected in the conception of sin. Whereas the Western mind defines sin as a violation of the divinely established legal relationship between God and man, the Eastern mind—influenced by Greek philosophy—defines it as a diminution of essence, a loss of substance, a wound or infection of the original image of God, the which man is and ought to be. Redemption, therefore, is not primarily the restitution of a legal relationship that has been upset by sin. Rather, it is fulfillment, renewal, transfiguration, perfection, deification of man's being.

[d] THE PRIMACY OF LOVE. We have already said that the idea of love rather than of justice dominates Eastern religiosity. A characteristic instance of this is St. John Chrysostom's catechetic sermon on the parable of the toilers in the vineyard (Matt. 20:1–16). In the Eastern Church this sermon is to this day read from all pulpits. It is a triumphal hymn of the victory of love. Awareness of the overflowing fullness of divine love drives away all thought of any schemes of reckoning and satisfaction. Divine grace is bestowed as generously upon those who are called in the eleventh hour as upon those who were called in the eighth and ninth hours. "Ye who are first and ye who are last, receive your reward. Rich and poor, rejoice together. Ye who are dutiful and ye who are neglectful, honor the day. Ye who have fasted and ye who have not fasted, today is

the day of your rejoicing. The table is laden; let all partake! The calf is fattened; let none depart hungry. All may partake in the feast of faith. All may partake of the wealth of goodness. Let none complain of poverty, for the kingdom for all is come. Let none mourn transgressions, for forgiveness has risen radiant from the grave. Let none fear death, for the Savior's death has freed us from death."

Such a pattern clearly excludes the doctrine of predestination. From the beginning, the Eastern Church secretly inclined toward the theory of universal salvation. Origen (†c. 254) had developed this idea in his theory of eons. The Judgment at the end of our eon will not be the ultimate judgment, will not forever set apart the saved and the damned. It will only assign men their place in a new age of the universe (eon) in which everyone will have a fresh chance to ascend to glory. At the end of all eons everything evil will have been winnowed out; the fallen angels and even Satan himself will turn back to the divine Logos. The Church officially disavowed this doctrine; nevertheless a hankering for it persisted within Eastern Orthodox religious thought, and Eastern theologians have repeatedly revived it.

The legalistic temper of Western Christianity has, characteristically, enlarged upon the idea of eternal damnation to a point quite alien to the Orthodox Church. Both Thomas Aquinas and Calvin in describing the bliss of the saved, suggest that one of the pleasures of heaven will consist in looking down upon the torments of the eternally damned, for do not these torments glorify divine justice? Such attitudes, following as they do from the legalistic thinking of the West, are not to be found in the work of Eastern religious thinkers. Similarly the Eastern Church has never thought of Judgment Day in the strictly juristic terms customary in the West. It does not haggle over anyone's right to salvation or insist upon an individual's achievements or the achievements of the Church's saints and martyrs. There is only confidence in grace and in the "love of man—

philanthropia," which is an attribute of the divine Logos. Confidence and, in addition, prayer for divine mercy.

For all these reasons the Orthodox Church could scarcely comprehend the theological principles of the Occidental Reformation, springing as these did from the need felt in the West for a religious approach based on a new interpretation of the doctrine of justification. The Reformers, of course, were attacking specific Roman Catholic doctrines and customs that Orthodoxy too had always rejected and fought—for example, papal primacy and the celibacy of the clergy. Here the Eastern Church was in full sympathy. But the central issue of justification interested only a few Orthodox theologians who had been educated in the West, such as Cyril Lukaris. These tried to insert the problem into Orthodox theology, but the grafted shoot soon withered.

In spite of this it would be wrong to view Eastern Orthodox and Western Christianity as absolutely antithetical to each other. A study of the liturgy and dogma of the East will reveal tendencies toward a legalistic view of the Church. The West, especially Roman Catholicism, can certainly claim its share of mystics. In fact, the history of the Western churches has been characterized by repeated renascences of mysticism. Recently, Roman Catholic theologians have given a great spur to the study of Orthodox liturgy and mysticism through exemplary editions and translations. Differences are more in the nature of nuances whereby the common tradition is given this or that alternate emphasis.

3. SOME PRINCIPAL DOGMAS

In what way have the individual dogmas been elaborated? Here we must go back to our earlier observation that all genuine faith is ultimately founded upon direct transcendental experiences. At the same time genuine faith has a natural impulse to clarify intellectually its underlying ideas. St. Augustine enunciated this principle as *Credo ut intellegam.* The modern reader is apt to be a stranger to this process by which religious experience develops into doctrine; he contents himself with accepting the existence of dogma as a historical fact. For this reason we shall illustrate the process in the cases of three fundamental dogmas of the Orthodox Church.

The Doctrine of the Trinity

The believers of the primitive Church had experienced the overwhelming reality of God in a threefold form. First, in the form of the Creator and Preserver of the universe, the Founder of the moral law, the Lord and Judge of nations and persons, the Lord of history, this was God as they knew him from the Old Testament. Second, they encountered God in the form of Jesus Christ, in the Son of God who had become Son of Man, in the incarnate Logos in whom they felt "the whole fullness of the presence of Deity." Third, they encountered God in the wonderful plenitude of the works of the Holy Spirit, whom they saw operative in their midst in the various gifts of prophecy, annunciation, power over demons, healing, dominion over the elements and the raising of the dead. The liturgical worship of God in the form of Father, Son and Holy Spirit sprang from this direct religious experience and became established long before theological reflection had formulated the dogma. Examples of Trinitarian liturgical phrases can already be found in the New Testament.

Nevertheless, theological clarification was absolutely essential, for the Jewish religion was based on uncompromising stress upon the oneness of God. How could the oneness of God, that cornerstone of both the Jewish and the Christian Scriptures, be reconciled with the fact that believers of Christian communities experienced God in this threefold aspect? This question appealed to the speculative bent of the Greek mind. In the course of the first few centuries of the Christian Church numerous solutions to the problem were proposed—so numerous that they comprise a branch of their own in the history of dogma. We cannot here trace all the steps of the discussion on the Trinity. In spite of all attempts at solution, the difficulty remained: in each particular case, members of the Christian community experienced the three-fold God in one of his individual forms, in one of the personal manifestations of Deity. The believers felt that they had met separately the Father, the Son and the Holy Spirit; they had distinct conceptions of the special qualities of each. The three manifestations had been concretely experienced, could be experienced by others, and therefore could not be wiped out by theological theorizing. And yet . . . was not God One?

The Orthodox Church as an institution did not attempt a rational solution of this problem. The dogma of the Church merely tried to fit the mystery of the divine Being within a certain conceptual framework. It was concerned only with fixing two points: the oneness of the nature of God and the individuality and particularity of the three forms in which God had manifested himself to believers in the course of history. Neoplatonic philosophy, with its metaphysics of substance and its doctrine of hypostasis, afforded a means for capturing these difficult points. The paradoxical combination of unity and trinity was summed up in the formula: "Three hypostases in one Being." The Neoplatonic concept of *hypostasis* was later clarified and replaced by *person,* a word taken over from the language of Roman law because it seemed a better term for the particularity and individuality of the three divine aspects.

The various theological proposals for the solution of the problem of the Trinity constitute one of the most magnificent intellectual feats in the history of thought. But it must not be forgotten that these efforts to interpret the divine mystery were not the work of philosophers, who operate primarily in the realm of logical processes. Rather, the figures involved were charismatic personalities, men endowed with the gifts of the Spirit. Their theological endeavors were closely connected with liturgy, meditation and contemplation. Many of them were practicing ascetics, and they expressed their insights as much in hymns as in theological treatises. Ultimately all such speculation terminated in worshipful praise of the mystery of the Holy Trinity. The first Trinity canon of Metrophanes runs:

Engendered from Thee, O Father, there radiated divinely without efflux, as Light forth from the Light, the immutable Son; out of Thee also proceeds the Spirit, the divine Light.

Believing, we adore the One Deity's three-personal glory; Him we praise. . . .

Since Thou art source and root, as Father Thou art as it were the primal ground of the Deity of like nature in the Son and Thy Holy Spirit.

Pour out to my heart Thy triple-sunned light and illuminate it by participation in the light that makes it like unto Divinity.

The Holy Threeness and undivided Nature, undividedly divided into three persons and remaining undivided in the essence of Deity, let us, the earthborn, venerate Thee in fear and praise Thee as creator and Lord, Thou God of surpassing goodness. . . .

As interpretations of the mystery of the Trinity grew, a striking difference sprang up in the course of time between the Orthodox and the Roman Catholic dogma. The point at issue was the question of the relationship of the Holy Spirit to the two other Persons within the divine Trinity. Biblical testimony offered only a single reference to the eternal procession of the Spirit from the Father. In that one reference the Spirit is distinctly differentiated from the temporal "sending" (John 14:26; 15:26) of the Spirit promised by Jesus during his mission upon earth. In the Eastern Church, the Father is regarded as the sole source and the sole First Cause both of the Son, who is begotten by the Father from eternity, and the Holy Spirit, who from eternity proceeds out of the Father.

By contrast, in the West the Spirit is held to proceed

from the Father and the Son. This doctrine has become established and has been interpolated into the Nicene Creed, which in its original form was accepted by both the Eastern and the Western churches. The original version taught only the procession of the Holy Spirit from the Father. In the ninth century, however, Charlemagne effected this revision of the doctrine despite the initial resistance of the Pope; by insertion of the word *filioque* (and the Son) the Latin version of the Creed thenceforth spoke of the procession of the Holy Spirit from the Father and the Son.

This tampering with the wording of Christendom's central Creed, which had its fixed place in the Eucharistic liturgy, and hence was familiar to every believer, seemed to the Greeks an assault upon the innermost substance of the religion itself. For the Creed was one of the most venerable formulas of the Church and had appeared inviolable in all its terms. In later polemics the theologians of the Eastern Church always pointed to this revision of the Creed as the most significant sign of the Roman Catholic Church's deviation from the Orthodox faith. Orthodox theologians, in fact, have attempted to explain the subsequent evolution—which they consider a degeneration—of both the Roman Catholic West and its dialectical opposition, the Protestant Reformation, as resulting from this wrong-headed interpretation of the dogma of the Trinity. They have gone so far as to dub the whole of western European culture a "culture of the *filioque*," that is, a culture stemming from this Western betrayal of the original verities of the religion.

In reality the question was hardly one of fundamental faith, as theologians in both East and West have since conceded. It was a philosophic conflict. The Eastern view was largely shaped by the tenets of Neoplatonic philosophy, the Son and the Holy Spirit being regarded as two hypostases proceeding from a single principle, from the single First Cause and Root of Deity. The West, following the example of St. Augustine, was rather seeking to describe the secret of the inner life in God.

The difference in point of view might be put this way: the original Orthodox wording places its stress upon the independence of the Holy Spirit as the vital force of the Church. Insofar as it does stress this, the Orthodox formula aptly expresses the charismatic experiences of the primitive Christian community. The Latin wording, on the other hand, provides a firmer conception of the unity of God's life as it manifests itself in a great variety of internal relations among the Persons of the Trinity. It also subordinates the *Pneuma* somewhat more to the institution of the Church, which is considered a creation of the Son. This is not necessarily heresy, nor need the two views be regarded as mutually exclusive antitheses.

The Christology

The dogmas concerning Jesus Christ also derive from spontaneous religious experiences of the primitive Church. The believers of the early Church had acknowledged Jesus as the incarnate and resurrected Son of God. They regarded the testimony of the disciples, who had witnessed the epiphanies, as proof that he was indeed the exalted Lord who sits at the right hand of the Father and would return in glory to bring about the fulfillment of his kingdom.

From the very beginning, however, several interpretations of the person of Jesus existed side by side. The Gospel of Mark, for example, implicitly views Jesus as a man upon whom the Holy Spirit descended at the time of the baptism in the Jordan and who was proclaimed, by God's voice from the clouds, to be the Son of God. The Christological theories that later grew out of the theological school of Antioch all followed along this line; they took the humanity of Jesus as their starting point and considered that his divinity lay in his consciousness of God, in the divine destiny that God had imposed upon him by an infusion of the Spirit.

But the Gospel of John presents another view. Here Jesus is primarily regarded as the incarnate divine Logos. Jesus is divine not because divinity has been conferred upon him from without, but because he is a preexistent celestial Being who descended into the world: the divine Logos who assumed a fleshly human body in order to affect human history. This theory dominated the Alexandrian school of theology. Thus a creative rivalry sprang up between the Antiochene and the Alexandrian schools, each school exerting an influence upon clergy, monks and laymen far beyond the boundaries of the respective cities. Nestorianism with its greater emphasis upon the human side of Jesus was an outgrowth of the Antiochene school; Monophysitism with its stress upon the divine nature of Christ grew out of the Alexandrian school.

The history of dogma records an endless series of intermediary solutions between the two extreme positions; it is impossible to go into them all here. As with the dogma of the Trinity, an astonishing plurality of views on the nature of Christ developed side by side. During the first three centuries of the Christian era the creeds of the various Christian communities differed considerably in their wording. When Christianity became the official religion of the Empire under Constantine, it became necessary to unify the varying views and set up a standard creed. The great ecumenical councils produced a succession of drafts in their efforts to create a unified formula that would be binding upon the whole Church throughout the Empire.

The Christological formulas of the Eastern Church do not try to provide a rationalistic explanation of the phenomenon of Christ. They aim to bring out at least the three aspects of the mystery of divine Sonship which the Church regarded as essential. First, the fact that Jesus Christ, Son of God, is God in full measure, that in him "the whole plenitude of Deity is present." Second, that he is man in full measure. Third, that these two "natures" do not exist unconnected side by side, but that they are joined within Christ in a personal unity. Here, too, Neoplatonic substance metaphysics supplied the intellectual categories for defining these theological concerns. Thus the concept of the sameness of substance—*homoousia*—of the divine Logos with God the Father guaranteed the full divinity of Jesus Christ. The mystery of the person of Jesus Christ could then be summed up in the formula: two natures in one person. Once again the concept of person derived from Roman law was useful for conveying the conception of the fully divine and fully human nature within a single entity.

What we have said concerning the development of Trinitarian doctrine also applies to the elaboration of the Christology: it was not the product of abstract logical operations but sprang from the liturgical and charismatic realm of prayer, meditation and asceticism. The dogma of Christ is not intended to be abstract theory; it is forever being reexpressed in the many hymns of the Eastern Church. The Easter liturgy puts it: "The King of Heaven appeared on earth out of sympathy for man and associated with men. For he took his flesh from a pure virgin and, assuming it, came out from her. One is the Son, twofold in substance but not as a person. Therefore, proclaiming him perfect God and perfect man in truth, we confess him Christ, our God."

The Dogmatic Position of the Mother of God

The dogma of the incarnation of the divine Logos is closely linked with the dogma of the Virgin Mary as "Mother of God" and "God-bearer." Again, the cult of the Mother of God did not develop out of theory; rather, the doctrine itself reflects only the extraordinary importance that veneration of the Mother of God early acquired in the liturgy, in the devotions of the Christian communities, and in the personal worship of Orthodox believers.

This birth of the cult of the Virgin Mary as "God-bearer"—*theotókos*—is one of the most amazing processes in the history of the primitive Church. The New Testament would seem to offer little stimulus for such a development. Mary appears in all four Gospels as playing only the most subsidiary of roles. It is disclosed that Jesus encountered considerable opposition from his family when he began to preach the kingdom of God. According to the Gospel of Mark, his family were so little convinced of his mission that they thought him insane (Mark 3:21). Mary does appear twice, without mention of her name, as the mother of Jesus; but Jesus himself consistently refuses to call her mother. He addresses her only as "Woman," which by Jewish standards was unusually insulting. The well-known words, "Woman, what have I to do with thee" (John 2:4), are probably the harshest expression of this deliberate detachment.

Nevertheless, the conception of Jesus Christ as the Son of God was early paralleled by a tendency in Christian communities to accord the Mother of God's Son a special position within the Church. There are hesitant intimations of this in the New Testament. Only Matthew and Luke mention the virgin birth—which does not fit in very logically with the preceding genealogy. Nevertheless, the idea of the virgin birth entered into the creeds of all Christendom and became one of the strongest motifs in the liturgy and worship of the early Church.

Veneration of the Mother of God took a tremendous leap from the moment Constantine made Christianity the official religion of the Empire and the pagan masses began pouring into the Church. For thousands of years the religious mentality of the peoples of the Mediterranean basin and the Near East had been shaped by the cult of the Great Mother Goddess and divine virgin. From the ancient popular religions of Babylonian Ishtar to the mystery religions of the late Hellenistic Age the Great Goddess had been worshiped under a variety of forms. The peoples who had practiced her cult could not easily adjust to the sole dominance of a Father God and to the strictly patriarchal structure of Judaic religiosity, which had been taken over by the early Christians. This ancient tradition sought a new mode of expression within the Christian Church and found it in adoration of the virginal Mother of God in whom the mysterious union of the divine Logos with human nature had been accomplished. Popular religious feeling elevated Mary to a place never originally allotted her by the Church.

In Egypt the veneration of Mary began very early. Origen, the Alexandrian Father of the Church, employed the term *theotókos*—God-bearer—in the third century. The Council of Ephesus gave its sanction to this title. The second Council of Constantinople added the epithet "everlasting Virgin." The prayers and hymns of the Orthodox Church invoke the name of the Mother of God as often as the names of Christ and the Holy Trinity. A good example of such homage is found in the Eucharistic liturgy of St. John Chrysostom, at the conclusion of the great intercessory prayer: "Truly worthy is it to praise Thee, God-bearer, eternally blessed and perfectly irreproachable Mother of our God, who art more worthy of honor than the cherubim and incomparably more glorious than the seraphim, who, intact, hast borne the Divine Logos—Thee, the true Mother of God, we praise."

A special feature of the Eastern Church is the doctrine of Heavenly Wisdom (*Sophia*). The concept of a personified "Heavenly Wisdom" is first to be found in Late Judaism. She is conceived of as a celestial being alongside God who serves as mediator of the work of creation and also as the mediator through whom God knows men. In Roman Catholic Mariology the Blessed Virgin Mary is identified with Heavenly Wisdom; that is to say, the process of deification of the Mother of God has gone a step further, Mary being equated with the divine hypostasis called Heavenly Wisdom. The Eastern Orthodox Church refrained from taking this further step. Despite its great veneration for the Mother of God, the Eastern Church never forgot the true grounds for that veneration: that through Mary the divine Logos had become incarnate.

In the theology, the liturgy and the minds of the people, the Mother of God and Heavenly *Sophia* were two separate entities. In iconography, too, the distinction was maintained: Heavenly Wisdom is usually represented together with her three daughters: Faith, Love and Hope. In the minds of the people the two doctrines are related only to the extent that *Sophia* occasionally appears as the cosmic aspect of the Mother of God, as a kind of entelechy of the universe, the intelligible world, the archetype of creation, comprehending the whole world in her ideal form and beauty. The great cathedral of *Hagia Sophia* in Constantinople, and the many other churches of that name, are dedicated to Heavenly Wisdom in this sense. In modern Russian religious philosophy, and chiefly in the works of Vladimir Soloviev, Pavel Florensky, V. N. Ilyin and Sergei Bulgakov an elaborate Sophiology has been developed; it has, however, met with strong opposition from the traditionalist Orthodox theologians.

Among the innumerable hymns in honor of the Mother of God in which her cosmic aspect is also touched upon, we shall quote only the hymn of the shepherds from the morning service of *Akathistos Saturday:*

Joy to Thee, Mother of the Lamb and the Shepherd.
Joy to Thee, Herder of spiritual sheep.
Joy to Thee, Avenger on invisible enemies.
Joy to Thee, Opener of the gates of Paradise.
Joy to Thee, Heaven rejoices with the earth.
Joy to Thee, earth dances with Heaven.
Joy to Thee, resounding Tongue of the Apostles.
Joy to Thee, unconquerable Courage of the victorious.
Joy to Thee, mighty Bulwark of Faith.
Joy to Thee, glorious Monument of Grace.
Joy to Thee, through Thee Hades was stripped.
Joy to Thee, through Thee we received the garb of glory.
Joy to Thee, virgin Bride.
Joy to Thee, Initiate of inscrutable counsels.

Joy to Thee, Warrant of them who crave rest.

Joy to Thee, Prelude of the wonder of Christ.

Joy to Thee, Perfection of His teachings.

Joy to Thee, heavenly Ladder, upon Whom God descended.

Joy to Thee, Bridge that leads from earth up to Heaven.

Joy to Thee, Glory oft-declared by the angels.

Joy to Thee, sore Wound of all devils.

Joy to Thee, Who inexpressibly hast received the Light.

Joy to Thee, Who hast taught no one the way of it.

Joy to Thee, overtowering the knowledge of the wise.

Joy to Thee, illuminating the senses of the faithful.

Joy to Thee, virgin Bride.

IV.

Constitution and Law of the Orthodox Church

1. THE ORIGIN OF THE CANON LAW

Rudolf Sohm, the well-known historian of Church law, came forth with the highly controversial thesis that the elaboration of canon law was the downfall of the early Church. The primitive Christian community had lived in a fellowship of love that sprang from experiencing the direct presence of the Holy Spirit, he said. With the development of canon law, the free, spontaneous operation of the Holy Spirit in the Church was repressed, and the inspired leadership was replaced by an elected, office-holding bureaucracy.

Seductive though it is, this idea of Sohm's cannot be sustained. The primitive Church was also ruled by law, for even the earliest communities wished to be guided by the apostles' instructions. The pastoral epistles of Paul virtually established the constitution of the Church. Moreover, the authority of the Holy Spirit transformed the inspired commands of the prophets within the Church into statutes of permanent validity. Spirit and law were not opposites; spiritual holiness created Sacred Law; the authority of the one upheld the authority of the other.

Simple logic also casts some discredit on this theory. We cannot imagine a church operating effectively by inner light alone. A historical community like the Christian Church, charged with the duty of making converts on a massive scale, could scarcely have functioned without a fixed legal organization.

2. THE THREE BULWARKS AGAINST HERESY

The problem of heresy was a further reason for the Church to set up fixed standards. Gnosticism and the religions of late antiquity had a powerful influence upon Christian theology and resulted in a great variety of interpretations of the Christian gospel. These pagan ideas were all the more insidious because their proponents likewise claimed divine inspiration or adduced revelations of the resurrected Christ. The Church set up three bulwarks against the flood of "pneumatic" prophetic and visionary notions, and against the tide of pagan syncretism. These three bulwarks were the canon of the New Testament, the Creed, and the apostolic succession of bishops. All three rested upon a common foundation: the idea of "apostolicity."

The Apostolic Canon

The official New Testament as we know it today was not so much a collection of existing writings, as a selection from them. The first few centuries of the Christian era were astonishingly productive of sacred writings: gospels, apocalypses and other prophetic works, and epistles. Gnosticism and pagan-Christian syncretism were responsible for much of this literary output. Out of the wealth of available material the Church eliminated everything that did not seem fully to accord with the apostolic tradition. The "apostolicity" of these writings was the criterion of selection.

The Orthodox Church has kept this fact in mind. It has

never forgotten that the Church created the New Testament. This is one of the essential differences between the Orthodox Church and the Reformed churches, for the latter regard Scripture as the ultimate criterion and authority for the Church and ecclesiastical dogma. The Orthodox Church knows that the Christian Church is older than the New Testament, that it existed for many decades without the New Testament. Its tradition is older than Scripture, in fact is the source of Scripture itself. Hence the importance of the apostolic tradition to the Eastern Church. Holy Scripture is regarded as only a special form of the apostolic tradition, namely, that form which has been fixed in writing.

The Apostolic Creed

A second, highly condensed summary of the beliefs of the Church, at first oral and later written, likewise arose out of the apostolic tradition. This was the apostolic Creed. It, too, was constructed to fend off Gnostic and syncretistic interpretations of the Christian truths. The most important root of the Creed was the liturgy, especially the baptismal liturgy. From the epistles of Paul and the pastoral letters we can see that even in the oldest communities the Christian evangel had coalesced into specific didactic formulas, used especially in conjunction with the Eucharist, but also included in the sacrament of baptism. The briefest of these didactic formulas was the profession of faith made at baptism; its wording was at first kept secret and imparted to the candidate only at the baptism itself.

In the early days of the Eastern Church there were a large number of these creeds, embodying the somewhat varying traditions of each of the great Christian communities. The decree of the Council of Nicaea in 325 for the first time set up a uniform creed. In 381, at the end of half a century of disputes over the interpretation of this Nicene Creed, it was accepted by the Synod of Constantinople with only the most minor changes. To this day the

Creed is recited at every Eucharistic service, in the baptismal liturgy, and at many other services and consecrations.

The Apostolic Succession of Bishops

The Church's third bulwark against free, ungovernable charisma and against the currents of Gnosticism and syncretism was the episcopal office, which was justified on grounds of apostolic succession. Missionary work, the period of persecutions, repression of free prophecy, and the struggle with Gnosticism and other heresies all served to swell the prestige of the monarchical episcopal office during the first few centuries of the Christian era. As the priest who conducted the Eucharistic services, as teacher and as pastor, the bishop became the chief spiritual guide of the community. He was regarded as *the* representative of the Church. His office was seen as a direct successor of the office of the apostles whom Christ himself had chosen; it was considered the symbol and guarantee of the unbroken continuity of the Church of Christ. For Christ himself had installed the first apostles and entrusted them with full spiritual powers; these apostles in turn appointed ministers for the congregations they had founded and imparted to them, by the sacramental laying on of hands, the powers and grace of their office; and these men in turn passed the office on to their successors in the same way. The apostolic succession insures the legitimacy of episcopal government of the Church, and the legitimacy of episcopal doctrine as well.

3. THE SOURCES OF CANON LAW

The principal sources of the Church's codified law are: first, Holy Scripture, especially the New Testament, from which the early Christians drew instructions on the structure, the sacramental and the marital practices of their communities; second, the oral tradition of the Orthodox

Church; third, Church customs, as long as they did not run counter to Scripture or oral tradition; fourth, the *canones* of the seven ecumenical councils recognized by the Orthodox Church; and the *Trullanum,* which was the supplement to the legislative work of the fifth and sixth ecumenical councils (Constantinople, 553 and 680–81). The *Trullanum* was a meeting held in Constantinople in 692 at which the Apostolic Canons of the fourth century were likewise ratified. In addition there are the decisions of various special synods and the decrees of the Fathers of the Church—especially Basil, Athanasius, Cyril of Alexandria, Gregory of Nazianzus and Gregory of Nyssa—and the pronouncements of famous ecclesiastical jurists of the Byzantine Middle Ages.

After the establishment of the state Church, the Byzantine emperors, and in later times the governments of the various Orthodox states, issued ordinances for the Church which had far-reaching effects upon canon law. Soon after the death of the Emperor Justinian the legal norms of the Orthodox Church were mustered along with state ecclesiastical laws into collections that usually went by the name of *Nomocanon.* These collections differ widely in the various national Orthodox churches. There is no one collection that is accepted by all the Orthodox churches as the *Codex Iuris Canonici* is accepted for the entire Roman Catholic Church. Bishops and councils of the Orthodox Church have a certain degree of freedom in their execution of canon law; they may apply the letter of the law to an individual case, or may avail themselves of their privilege of dispensation. Nowadays the entire Orthodox Church recognizes the necessity for a reform of the canon law, parts of which apply only to long-outmoded conditions. Nevertheless, the individual Orthodox churches to this day cling to the traditional formulation of the law; where difficulties in its application arise, they try to solve the dilemma by dispensation.

4. THE CONSTITUTIONAL PRINCIPLE
OF THE CHURCH

The Orthodox Church acknowledges the monarchical principle as far as the whole Church is concerned, this concept embracing both the visible Church on earth and the invisible celestial Church. The master, lord and sole head of the Church is Christ. But the monarchical principle does not in practice rule the organization of the visible Church. Here purely democratic principles prevail. No single member of the Church is considered to have a legal position fundamentally superior to that of the other members. Even the clergy, aside from the sacramental powers accorded to them by their consecration, have no special rights that would set them above the laity. The Orthodox Church prizes this democratic principle as one of its oldest traditions. Just as all the apostles were equal in rank and authority, so their successors, the bishops, are all equal.

It is true that the principle of the so-called monarchical episcopate became established quite early in the primitive Church. That is to say, the bishop was recognized as holding the leading position within the Church. But this did not mean that he alone represented the entire spiritual power of the Church. Not even the bishops as a body constituted the highest authority of the Church. This was vested in the ecumenical consensus or conscience of the Church, which meant the general opinion of clergy and laymen taken together. Even the decision of an ecumenical council acquires validity only if it is accepted by this general consensus of the whole Church. Although the bishop represents the unity of the Christian community and exercises full spiritual powers, he is no autocrat; he and all the clergy subordinate to him are regarded as parts of the entire *ecclesia,* the living organism of which Christ is the head.

At the present time the government of the Orthodox churches is markedly synodal in character. Laymen as well

as priests may take part in Orthodox synods. Election to
ecclesiastical offices also takes place at synods, and the
laity participate. This election rule holds true for parish
priests as well as for bishops and patriarchs. The constitu-
tions of the various national Orthodox churches differ in
the degree to which the state intervenes in ecclesiastical
government. Thus the Holy Synod of the Russian Orthodox
Church, which Peter the Great set up, was less an ecclesiastical council than an organ of the state directed by
an absolutistic ruler. In the constitution of the Greek Orthodox Church certain rights are accorded to the King of
Greece. In general the synodal or council system has
gained more importance during the past several centuries.
"The tendency for the collaboration of clergy and people
in the administration of the Church, which has become
characteristic of the Orthodox Church during the past hundred years, cannot be regarded as a product of modern
democracy; rather, it represents a revival of the primitive
Christian principle that bishops, clergy and people form an
indissoluble vital unit" (Heiler).

Major questions of faith, rites and canon law are
theoretically put before an ecumenical council. This is an
assemblage of all the Orthodox bishops who decide these
questions by majority vote. There have been seven great
ecumenical councils: Nicaea in 325, Constantinople in 381,
Ephesus in 431, Chalcedon in 451, Constantinople II in 553,
Constantinople III in 680 and Nicaea II in 787. No ecumenical councils have taken place since, though many questions of faith, dogma and ritual have arisen since the
eighth century which theologians feel urgently require regulation. But the breakup of Eastern Orthodoxy into various
old and new types of ecclesiastical patriarchates and independent churches, and the tragic involvement of Orthodoxy
in the political disasters of past centuries, have so far
dashed all hopes for any new ecumenical council. Only
recently, fresh efforts have been made to organize such a
council.

The synodal system of the Orthodox Church has undergone many strains in the course of history. Holders of one or another prominent see have sought to dominate the Church. The rivalry among the various Orthodox patriarchates sprang partly from this struggle for hegemony within the Church. When the Orthodox Church became the official Church of the Byzantine Empire, it was only in the nature of things that the Patriarch of Constantinople should find himself in a special role. In terms of the synodal government of the Church this primacy was only an honorary one, but for centuries the patriarchs of Constantinople repeatedly tried to transform their honorary primacy into a legal one and to secure papal privileges for themselves. Their claims, however, were never generally recognized. To this day the patriarch is regarded only as *primus inter pares*. That is, he is first among the holders of the old and new patriarchates of the East, but he is not head of the entire Orthodox Church with any legal title to primacy. Even the honorary primacy is not uncontested; when the All-Russian Synod of Moscow was called in 1948, Russian Orthodox canonists questioned the right of the Ecumenical Patriarch to call an ecumenical council. This right, they contended, was vested in the Patriarch of Moscow.

In contradistinction to the Roman Church, the Orthodox Church permits marriage for its priests, but this marriage must take place before the priest receives his consecration. Second marriage after the death of a priest's wife is forbidden. The widower priest is confronted with the alternative of either returning to the laity or becoming a monk. In practice, therefore, every candidate for spiritual office must decide before consecration whether he will take a wife or become a monk. This decision is all the more weighty because canon law dictates that bishops must be celibate. Hence bishops can come only from the monastic order. This rule has had two crucial consequences for the entire Orthodox clergy. The first is that the married priests cannot rise to higher ecclesiastical offices. Therefore it became customary for priests not to be given an academic theological education; they were trained in seminaries in which instruction was limited largely to conduct of the liturgy. Higher theological education at religious academies was reserved for members of the monastic order who alone could become leaders of the Church. Thus a great educational gulf came into being between the higher and the lower clergy, a gulf that was all the wider because the Orthodox priest was so ill paid. Inadequate education and poor pay made for the low social position of the priests as a class in many Orthodox countries. Only in very recent times, chiefly in the Greek Church, have there been successful efforts to raise the spiritual and social level of the priesthood. More far-reaching reforms are still in abeyance. The Communist revolutions in various Orthodox countries have dealt severe blows to the structure of the Church. To meet these new conditions there has been a movement to change canon law so as to remove the distinction between the "black" and the "white" clergy and to allow married priests to rise to the episcopate. So far all such attempts have failed.

V.

National Churches, Schismatic Churches, Emigrant Churches

1. ORGANIZATIONAL DIVERSITY OF THE ORTHODOX CHURCH

Today's Orthodox Church is composed of a number of highly diverse members. Alongside the old independent patriarchal churches of Constantinople, Alexandria, Antioch and Jerusalem there exist a number of old national churches such as the Catholicate of Georgia and the Church of Cyprus. There are also the monastic republic of Athos, with its peculiar and highly democratic constitution, and the Church of Sinai, likewise a product of monasticism. On Slavic soil there arose between the ninth and thirteenth centuries the Bulgarian Church, the Serbian Church and the Church of the Duchy of Kiev; an attempt to found a Slavic Church in the Moravian kingdom failed. After the nineteenth-century wars that liberated the Balkan peoples from their Turkish overlords, new national Orthodox churches were founded in the new Balkan states. More such national churches were born at the end of the First World War when the Baltic countries set up independent governments. Thus the Latvian, Lithuanian, Estonian and Finnish Orthodox churches came into being only after 1918, as did the Czechoslovak and Polish Orthodox churches.

Finally, there are the numerous Orthodox churches that were established in North and South America during the nineteenth century (see p. 83). Churches also grew up as an aftermath of the Bolshevist Revolution, when the Soviet Union persecuted and sought to exterminate the Russian Church and large numbers of Russian Orthodox exiles settled in various cities of Europe and Asia Minor. Important centers of Orthodox theological studies also arose in places where heretofore the faith had scarcely taken foothold. Existing exile churches were once more dispersed after the Second World War, when ecclesiastical leaders and theologians in the Balkans, Poland and Czechoslovakia fled before the invading Red Army.

To describe these many Orthodox churches would be beyond the scope of a work of this sort. But we must say something about the principles that permitted the formation of such variegated church organizations within Orthodoxy.

2. PRINCIPLES OF ORGANIZATION

The non-Orthodox observer is somewhat bewildered by the diversity he finds beneath the roof of Orthodoxy. To understand it, we must free our minds of a common preconception about the primitive Church. Most people imagine that institutional, organizational, dogmatic and liturgical uniformity prevailed in the Christian Church from the beginning. This idea, based as it is on the example of the present-day Roman Catholic Church, is historically false. The early centuries of the Church were marked by great variety in constitution, liturgy and dogma, variety even in regard to the canon of the New Testament. A trend toward uniformity appeared only after Constantine made the Christian Church the state church of the *Imperium*

Romanum. The councils held under the Empire were the most important instruments for achieving that uniformity. Before Constantine the major Christian communities in East and West had their individual creeds, their individual liturgies, their individual systems of doctrine, their treasure of special traditions in all realms of life. And this individuality and variety was a living creative process, which was far from having reached its end by the fourth century.

Linguistic and National Organization

Linguistic differentiation was especially striking and had the blessing of the Church itself. From the early days of the Church the Pentecostal miracle, when the Spirit conferred the "gift of tongues" upon the apostles, was regarded as a divine sanctioning of differences in language. Such differences were to be the means for spreading word of the kingdom of God (see p. 105 ff.). And in the course of history, nationalism has been one of the most potent forces in engendering variety within the Orthodox Church. The principle of bringing the gospel and the liturgy to each people in its own language led to the establishment of numerous national churches, each one restricted to the nationality in question. The oldest of these national churches, the Syrian Church, had already been formed before the end of the first century. Other national churches arose, many of which were later to profess divergent doctrines. Under this heading come the Armenian, Coptic, Ethiopian, Persian and Indian churches. The Georgian Church was also intermittently of this category.

The tendency toward individualization of the churches by their espousal of different languages, doctrines and liturgy was, then, implicit in the original Christian missionary work. But other forms of differentiation arose as a result of political conditions.

The development of Orthodoxy in all the various nation-states was characterized by a close relationship between Church and state. Each of the national churches had its independent supreme head. Thus the ecclesiastical organization in the Balkans during the early and late Middle Ages took an active part in the dramatic struggle between the Bulgarian and Serbian kingdoms and the Byzantine Empire; thus Kiev was the capital of the secular ruler and the seat of the metropolitan of the Rus kingdom, as Moscow was later to be the capital of the tsars and the seat of the Patriarch of Moscow. After the Greeks won their liberation from the Turks, an autonomous Greek national church was formed, whose metropolitan had his seat in Athens, the capital of the new King of Greece. Similarly the Bulgarian Church, first established in 864 by Tsar Boris I, was revived as an autonomous church along with the national rebirth of Bulgaria during the wars of liberation of the nineteenth century. The fate of the Serbian Church was linked with the drama of Serbia's fight for political independence; after the establishment in 1920 of the Kingdom of the Serbs, Croats and Slovenes (Yugoslavia), a Serbian patriarchate was set up in Belgrade. With the establishment of an independent Albanian state in 1914, measures were taken to create an "autocephalous" (i.e., "self-headed") Albanian Orthodox Church. Similarly the Finnish Orthodox Church came into being after Finland's declaration of independence; the Estonian, Lithuanian and Latvian national churches likewise were established along with the respective states after 1918. An Orthodox Polish Church was revived along with a reconstituted Poland between 1916 and 1918, though it was to be subjected to intense persecution by the Roman Catholic majority. After the founding of the Czechoslovak Republic in 1920 the Czech Orthodox national church was formed. In Romania there was something of a time lag; the union of all Romanians to form a national state took place in 1918, but the formation of a Romanian patriarchate did not come until 1925.

The intimate union of Church and state meant that the Orthodox churches of these countries were painfully af-

fected by the constant revision of frontiers in Europe. The
recent reshuffling of borders resulting from the incorpora-
tion of large areas of eastern Poland, Czechoslovakia and
Romania into the USSR, and the other territorial changes
that followed the Second World War, imposed grave strains
upon the relatively young autocephalous churches of northeast and southeast Europe.

Political Factors in Church Organizations

The Church inherited a second element of differentiation from the political organization of the Roman Empire.
The old patriarchates of Alexandria and Antioch arose out
of the division of the Roman Empire into provinces. When
the Empire itself split into western and eastern halves, the
old capital became the seat of the patriarchate of Rome
while the new capital of the Roman Empire became the
seat of the patriarchate of Byzantium. The bishops of Rome
and Byzantium continually sought to extend their claims
to ecclesiastical dominion over the entire Empire. Meanwhile the two other patriarchs bent all their energies upon
preserving their autonomy, and retaining control of their
large ecclesiastical provinces. Alexandria was the provincial capital of Egypt. Its bishop early exercised his ecclesiastical sway over the whole of Egypt, and under the
leadership of such great personalities as Athanasius, ecclesiastical centralism developed earlier in the Egyptian
Church than in Rome itself. The scope of the Bishop of
Rome, at least at first, went only as far as the suburbicar-
ian dioceses—areas within about one hundred miles of
Rome. The Bishop of Antioch, too, commanded far larger
territories than his Roman counterpart. Antioch was the
capital of the Roman province of Syria, but from the beginning the Antiochene Church had served as the headquarters for Christian missions to the east and northeast,
to Mesopotamia, eastern Asia Minor, the Caucasus,
Persia and Arabia, Siberia and China. However, in the
course of time Antioch was deprived of a great part of its

original missionary territory, when one by one the churches of those areas were parted from the mother church by political changes and dogmatic disagreements.

3. THE OLD "SCHISMATIC" CHURCHES

The splintering-off of the old so-called "schismatic" churches was brought about by both political and dogmatic causes. In considering this matter we must again remember the multiplicity of forms in the early Church. Uniformity could be achieved only by enthroning one of the existing types as orthodox and branding the others as heretical.

Constantine the Great had transformed the Christian Church, hitherto the Roman Empire's most dangerous foe, into an agency for restoring the unity of the Empire, for he rightly recognized that any such unity had to be founded on a spiritual and religious basis. Thus the unity of the Church became a political factor of the first importance. Unity of the Church had to be imposed for the sake of unity of the Empire, and Constantine and his successors bent every effort to enforce it. In the ensuing struggle all the rival factions strove above all to gain the emperor's ear. The victorious party could have opponents declared heretics and condemned as enemies of the state.

From that time forth, the unity of the Imperial Church coincided with the limits of the Empire's power; in East and West unity ended and multiplicity began where the political arm of Byzantium was no longer strong enough. The special course taken by the Church of Rome, whose bishops sought to enforce their claims to primacy with the aid of the young barbarian kingdoms of the North, was possible only because Rome lay outside the sphere of Byzantium's political power.

The fact that ecclesiastical factions that quarreled with an edict of the Imperial Church were declared heretical, and their members persecuted as enemies of the state, led to an inextricable mingling of ecclesiastical and political elements. We shall mention only two of the numerous consequences: Either the leaders of the minorities emigrated into enemy states bordering on the Byzantine Empire and established centers from which they combated the Byzantine Imperial Church and its theology, the while subverting local churches that were outside the direct control of the Empire; or despite the pronouncement against them, the leaders of such dissident groups stood their ground and collected so strong and loyal a body of followers that the authorities of the Empire were not able to impose their will upon them. Such groups had a better chance of withstanding pressure if they were established in border areas threatened by external enemies.

The Nestorian Church

The Nestorians were an example of the first type of dissidence. When the Imperial Church decided officially against the Christology of Patriarch Nestorius of Constantinople, his followers emigrated to eastern Syria and Persia. They impressed their theological views upon the Persian Church. The ideological breach was followed by organizational separation; the Persian Church broke with the patriarchate of Antioch. Persia, the archenemy of Byzantium, adapted an ecclesiastical structure antagonistic to the Church of the Byzantine Empire. Missions sent out from Edessa in eastern Syria, and later from Persia, operated throughout India and central Asia, China, Mongolia and southern Siberia (see p. 126 ff.).

The Monophysite Churches

The Monophysite churches are an example of the second type of resistance. Not only theological factors but national and racial ones played their part in the genesis of these churches. Monophysite doctrine emphasized the divine nature of Jesus Christ almost to the point of excluding his human nature. Adherents of this view had won the majority at the "Robber Council" of Ephesus in the year 449 and had succeeded in foisting their interpretation upon the theology of the whole Imperial Church. But only two years later the Council of Chalcedon condemned their doctrine as heretical. The two theological parties were so evenly divided in numbers and strength that the doctrine of Chalcedon could not win out either. The condemnation of the Monophysites led to a split, the Armenian, Coptic (Egyptian), Ethiopian, and the larger part of the Syrian and the Mesopotamian churches adhering to Monophysitism. Doctrine alone was not the sole divisive factor, for all these churches had already developed an independent church life in their own languages.

The influence of "non-theological" factors in turning the Egyptian Church to Monophysitism are particularly patent. The Monophysite doctrine was the logical outgrowth of views on the nature of Christ which had been advocated by the old theological school of Alexandria. At the Council of Ephesus in 431, Patriarch Cyril I of Alexandria had professed his belief in a Jesus Christ possessing only one, namely a divine, nature. When the Council of Chalcedon condemned this doctrine, Egyptian nationalism was offended. Significantly enough the native Copts rather than the Egyptian Hellenes were most strongly wedded to traditional Monophysite ideas. Factional feeling was intensified by the strains between the Copts and the Greeks, who were the economic and intellectual leaders of Egypt. A further element was the traditional rivalry between Alexandria, with its ancient claims to ecclesiastical primacy, and Constantinople—the Alexandrians regarding the latter as a parvenu city in Church affairs. The enmity between the churches was deepened by Byzantium's belated efforts to install Orthodox patriarchs of Greek origin in place of the banished Monophysite bishops. The native Copts deeply resented this. The conflict ultimately benefited the Moslem Arabs, for a good many of the Monophysite Copts hailed them as liberators from the yoke of Byzantine Orthodoxy.

Once entrenched in Egypt the Arabs oppressed the Copts and forced the religion of Islam upon them.

Because it had ties with the Egyptian Church dating back to the early missions, the Ethiopian Church has remained Monophysite to the present day.

Centralism and Particularism in the Orthodox Church

Throughout the history of the Orthodox Church, the tendency of the linguistic and national branches to split off into autocephalous national churches was a source of constant instability. These churches were always straining against the unifying aims of the Byzantine Church. Until the Turks captured Constantinople in 1453, the Byzantine Church was forever struggling to prevent the formation of new, independent national churches and maintain jurisdiction over the outlying territories. Where this proved impossible, Constantinople made an effort at least to keep the strategic ecclesiastical positions in the hands of Byzantine Greeks. In many Slavic churches, for example, stubborn battles developed between the Greek and the native clergy for possession of the most important episcopal seats and other influential church posts. The linguistic contention between Slavic and Greek liturgy in the Serbian, Bulgarian and Romanian churches was never wholly settled. In the Oriental provinces of the Church also, the rivalry between the Byzantine-minded Greeks and the native ecclesiastics produced constant tensions and at times open conflicts.

The Position of the Ecumenical Patriarch in the Ottoman Empire

Curiously enough the Byzantine Imperial Church was in a better position to exert authority when, after the downfall of the Byzantine Empire, it came under Turkish overlordship. The Turkish conquest strengthened rather than weakened the power of the Ecumenical Patriarch, for the Sublime Porte accepted him as the representative—in secular matters, too—of all Orthodox believers in the Turkish

Empire. Consequently he was legally invested with a number of political and civil rights over the Christian citizens of the realm. In practice this meant that the Sublime Porte accorded to the Patriarch of Constantinople rights far exceeding those he had exercised before the conquest. The centuries-old disputes between Byzantium and the separatistic Balkan churches were decided unequivocally in favor of the former; the provincial churches were officially placed directly under the jurisdiction of Constantinople.

The Byzantine patriarchs took advantage of this new legal position to establish a Greek cultural hegemony throughout their ecclesiastical territories. Once again the episcopal seats in the Balkan churches were occupied by Greeks; the Greek liturgy was restored and Greek theologians were charged with the training of the clergy. The various national churches were by no means pleased by this monopolistic state of affairs. The moment they succeeded in shaking off the Turkish yoke in the nineteenth century, they likewise overthrew the artificial hellenization and the jurisdictional hegemony of the Byzantine patriarch. National independence was accompanied by ecclesiastical independence. The nineteenth-century struggles between the Byzantine and the Bulgarian churches represented the climax in the long strife between the unifying tendencies of the Byzantine Greek Church and the nationalistic, racial principle in ecclesiastical matters.

The Emigrant Orthodox Churches

The numerous Orthodox churches in exile owe their particular character to the special conditions under which each specific group went into exile. During the nineteenth and twentieth centuries numerous Orthodox believers, members of various national churches, emigrated to America. Even where these emigrants assimilated quickly in language and customs, they clung to their national church affiliation as the cornerstone of their culture. In the United States and Canada, and in South America, particularly in Brazil and

Argentina, Orthodox church organizations of Russians, Ukrainians, Greeks, Serbs, Bulgarians, Romanians, Syrians and Arabs sprang into being. These formed the center of the respective emigrant groups, and the strong clannish ties of their members deeply affected their mode of life. In Brazil, for example, the Orthodox Syrians came to be the rich business element in the large cities. The manner in which these emigrant churches were linked with their home churches was again highly individual. Some home churches, such as the patriarchates of Antioch and Alexandria, attempted to maintain exarchates of their own on American soil. For the most part, however, these Orthodox emigrant churches struck out on their own paths. Sometimes they would unite to form new groupings. With new waves of immigration to the United States, new Orthodox church organizations were often set up, each of which would reflect the principal problems of ecclesiastical and general politics in the home church at the time of emigration.

VI.

Monasticism

1. BEGINNINGS OF MONASTICISM IN THE EARLY CHURCH

There is a common misconception that monasticism developed in the early Church after the persecutions ended. According to this view, it was a movement to counter the secularization that crept in once Christianity had become the official Church of the Roman Empire, with a resultant mass membership. This idea is quite inaccurate. The beginnings of monasticism go back to the very origins of Christendom. Most of the features characteristic of later monasticism were to be found in the oldest Christian communities. Common property, poverty and celibacy are apostolic ideals that are preached in the New Testament. Unmarried ascetics, both men and women, were early recognized by the Church as a special class; even in the epistles of Paul the ideal of celibacy is highly praised. The ascetically inclined Christians formed the core and the elite of the Christian fellowship; they were the cement that held the group together. In theology Clement of Alexandria (c. 150–c. 210) and Origen (c. 185–c. 254), the heads of the Alexandrian catechetical school, forged that curious conjunction of asceticism and mysticism which was to become the intellectual basis for later monasticism.

The word monk—*monachos*—originally did not mean, as is generally assumed, a hermit or solitary. Its primary meaning is "the unique one." The oldest Syrian term for monk, *ihidaja,* is even more unequivocal; it means simultaneously "the unique one" and "the perfect one." Within the Christian community the monk was originally "the perfect one" who strove to fulfill the evangelical commandment: "You therefore must be perfect, as your heavenly Father is perfect" (Matt. 5:48). The Syrian word likewise means "the only begotten." The Messianic title of Christ as the only-begotten Son (John 1:14) was thus carried over to the perfect Christian, the monk. He was the image of Jesus Christ and, being so, was exalted to the rank of an only-begotten son of God.

2. EREMITISM

Ascetics early took to living outside the community and outside the urban settlements, in solitary places and walled-off areas. After this development had become common, the meaning of the word monk acquired the additional sense of one living apart. The way of life pursued by these monks was obviously influenced by the precedent of older Hellenistic and Jewish religious communities, such as the monkish groups of Pythagoreans and the Essenes, of whom we have only recently learned through the discovery of the Dead Sea Scrolls and the excavations of an Essene community in Palestine.

Monasticism became an established institution of the Christian Church during the fourth century, at a time when the ascetic currents throughout the Church were gaining strength. This growing asceticism has been looked upon as a sign of the general pessimism, the world-weariness and decadence of late antiquity. The reality was just the opposite. The spread of asceticism was directly related to the spread of Christianity in the fourth century; it emerged not out of the population of the declining Empire, but out of the vigorous rural peoples of Egypt and Syria. The explanation must be sought in the thing itself: asceticism became more ascetic because there was a growing enthusiasm for it. The ascetics found that they could not shut themselves off from other men as much as they desired as long as they lived in the vicinity of populated places. In the search for greater isolation they moved into tombs, into abandoned and tumbledown homes and villages, into caves, and finally into the "great desert." Here they were excellently situated to carry out their principal task, the struggle with devils; for the solitude of the desert was regarded as the true dwelling place of demons, the refuge to which the old pagan gods had retreated before triumphantly advancing Christianity. Thus the spread of Christianity in Egypt and the fourth-century rise of monasticism in that country were two aspects of the selfsame process. Because the reversal of imperial religious policy had sent masses of new converts pouring into the churches, the number of those who sought perfection naturally increased; and these resolute warriors of Christ betook themselves to the desert. Sociologically speaking, this ascetic trend was a tremendous countermovement on the part of the Christian rural population against the moral decay of urban society in the late Empire—that decay which is plain to see in the literary and historical documents of the period.

The Church itself supported this movement to the best of its ability. *The Life of St. Antony,* by Athanasius of Alexandria (c. 295–373), the most important bishop of his day, represents the hermit's fearful struggle against demons in the desert as the model of a life of Christian perfection. This book meant more than the sanctioning of monasticism by the Church; it was official propaganda for the institution. It inspired innumerable Egyptian and Syrian Christians to depart for the solitude of the desert, there to strive for lives of perfection in spite of all demons. The eremitic movement of the fourth and fifth centuries, then, was nothing new; it was a variant of the kind of monasticism that had already existed in the primitive Church, the sole difference being that the "unique ones" lived in waste places remote from the communities of their fellow Christians.

3. MONASTERIES

Yet even these solitary battlers against devils did not remain alone. The hermits in the desert gradually gathered into more tightly organized fellowships who accepted the leadership of some spiritually eminent monk and met together for divine services, to exchange thoughts for the good of their souls, to instruct one another in Holy Scripture, and for meditation. A further step was taken when the hermits enclosed their small, usually conical, tentlike huts within a wall or a fence. Such enclosure brought with it the necessity for regulating the labor of the individual monks. The original form of the monastery in the East was not a common building with many cells united under one roof, but an assemblage of hermits' huts within a fenced area: architectural expression of the bridge between the ideal of solitude and the ideal of community life.

Pachomius (c. 292–346), a former Roman soldier, created the first monastery in the sense we give to the term today, gathering the monks together. About the year 320 he founded the first real monastery in Tabennisi, north of Thebes in Egypt; thirty to forty monks lived together in their clustered huts, each group under their own head. This same Pachomius established a monastic rule also, although it served more to regulate the physical life of the monastery than to provide spiritual guidance. The rule of Pachomius spread rapidly, even outside Egypt; monastic communities of the type he originated were soon to be found in Ethiopia. Bishop Athanasius of Alexandria, during his exile from 340 to 346, brought the rule to the West. Mar Awgin introduced the Pachomian monastic rule into Mesopotamia around the middle of the fourth century. St. Jerome made use of it when he established his monastery in Bethlehem in 404. The rule of Benedict of Nursia, which was so enormously to affect the character of Western monasticism, was likewise influenced by the rule of Pachomius.

The final shaping of monastic community life and the clearest statement of its nature and principles must be credited to Basil the Great (c. 330–79). His treatises on asceticism, originally written for the monks of Cappadocia, provided the theological and pedagogical foundation for cenobitism,[1] the community life of monks. He was the creator of the monastic rule that, although it underwent many changes and modifications, later became the standard one for Orthodox monasticism.

4. DIFFERENCE BETWEEN EASTERN ORTHODOX AND ROMAN CATHOLIC MONASTICISM

Down to the present day, Orthodox monasticism has faithfully preserved its fundamental union of asceticism and mysticism and has remained close to the monasticism of the primitive Church. This is not true of Roman Catholic monasticism, which has undergone two types of special development which have led it far from primitive monasticism.

The first is clericalization. In Roman Catholic monasteries today, the monks, with the exception of the serving brothers (*fratres*), are ordained priests. Thus they are involved with the sacramental tasks of the Roman Church as their predecessors were not. In the beginning the monks were laymen. In fact Pachomius expressly forbade monks to become clerics on the ground that "it is good not to desire dominion and fame." Basil the Great, however, introduced a special monastic oath and a special liturgical

[1] *Koinobios* (Gk.) = living in community.

ceremony for entry into a monastic order. The monks ceased to be pure laymen and assumed a middle position between clergy and laity. To this day, however, the greater part of the monks of the Orthodox Church are lay monks. In each monastery there are only a few fathers who are ordained priests—hieromonks—and therefore competent to administer the sacraments.

The second special feature of Roman Catholicism is the functional division of the monastic orders, which flowed logically out of clericalization. The various orders became auxiliary troops of the Church in its different fields of activity, such as the combating of heresy, missionary work, education, care of the sick. Roman Catholic monastic orders also show an extraordinary sociological range: there are knightly orders and mendicant orders, orders of distinctly feudal and aristocratic character alongside purely middle-class orders. Insofar as the orders in the West devoted themselves more and more to special missionary or pedagogical ends, to theological scholarship or ecclesiastical politics, they spent less time upon their original activities of prayer, meditation and contemplation. As the orders assumed functions the individual monks became functionaries. Nothing of the sort took place within the Eastern Church. The Orthodox Church has only a single monastic order, the order of "Basilians." It has only a single type of monastic habit, the long black rhason with the tall, black, rimless felt hat called the kamelaukion. It has only a single form of liturgy. Certain differences in the mode of life and constitution of individual monasteries have, however, developed in the course of centuries.

5. MONASTICISM
IN THE BYZANTINE IMPERIAL CHURCH

The Palestinian hermitages were organized by Hilarion of Gaza (†371) and Chariton the Great (†350), when they set up a community life for the isolated ascetics of the region. These hermitages became cenobitic monasteries which were called lauras. Other organizers and promoters of cenobitism on the soil of Palestine were Euthymios the Great (†473) and especially Abbot Sabas (439–532). The latter was the author of a monastic rule that was to exercise an enormous influence on Russian monasticism. The works of Cyril of Skythopolis (c. 515–58) on these illustrious fathers of monasticism are among the finest writings in early Christian literature and tell us a great deal about the daily life of the early monks. During the fifth century, monasticism also took root in Syria and on the Sinai Peninsula. Such great Syrians as Ephraem (306–c. 373) and Isaac (seventh century), John Climacus (c. 570–649) and Simeon Stylites the Elder (c. 390–459) illustrate the heights to which ascetic renunciation and mystic theology were brought.

In the period between the fourth and sixth centuries Eastern monasticism became one of the most vital factors in the Eastern Church. A good deal of the legislation of the Emperor Justinian (527–65) was concerned with the regulation of monastic organization. The eighth and ninth centuries were the period of the iconoclastic controversy, which might be considered a test of strength between the monastic orders and other elements of society. The monks were totally committed to the veneration of icons. The iconoclastic emperors used all the resources of political power to suppress the practice, but the pro-image party ultimately prevailed. This victory on the part of the monastic orders in turn strengthened the position and importance of monasticism in the Church. Those stormy years also saw the emergence of a great leader who became a key figure in the history of Orthodox monasticism, Theodore of Studion (†826). He was not only the most vigorous ideological spokesman for Orthodoxy in the iconoclastic controversy, but also one of the principal supporters of cenobitic monasticism. He was the founder of a monastic rule that was adopted by many new foundations as they sprang up throughout the realm subsequently dominated by the Orthodox Church, including the Slavic lands.

After the end of the iconoclastic controversy, monasticism in the East entered upon its most glorious period. The number of monasteries steadily increased, and monks gained so much influence that contemporaries referred to Byzantium as the "realm of the monks" and to the whole era as the "era of monkish glory."

6. RUSSIAN MONASTICISM

Eremitism and Cave Monasteries

In the East Slavic lands, monasticism had existed even before the conversion of Russia under Vladimir. Iconoclasm with its official persecution of monasticism had made many Orthodox monks flee from Byzantium and Asia Minor to Taurica and the Crimea. St. Stefan the Younger (†765), a zealous advocate of the veneration of images, refers to the northern shore of the Black Sea as the safest refuge for persecuted monks, who settled down in the many caves of the Crimean Mountains. These exiles brought their impassioned veneration of images to Russia. The flight to the Crimea and southern Russia meant, for the monks, a kind of relapse into the older forms of eremitism. Thus there developed in southern Russia, the Crimea, and also on the lower Don, during the eighth and ninth centuries, the beginnings of a type of cave monasticism that was later to be revived in the most famous of all cave monasteries, the Pecherskaya Laura of Kiev.

The latter was the product of ascetic ardor on the part of a number of pious souls of the lower classes. The monks of this institution won great esteem among their contemporaries by their devotion to "tears, fasting and praying." An old chronicle traces the origins of this monastery to the cleric who first dug a cave there. His name was Ilarion and he was, as the chronicler writes, "a good man, learned, and a faster." While still priest of the church in Brestovo, southwest of Kiev, he had dug a small cave for himself on a wooded hill on the right bank of the Dnieper to be used as a place for prayer and meditation. He was later appointed by Duke Yaroslav to be the first metropolitan of Russian origin. After this promotion Ilarion was hardly able to make these retreats, but the cave was soon taken over by one Antony (†1073), from the city of Lubech, near Chernigov. Others followed his example and soon there was a large colony of cave dwellers in the area. These individual ascetics were federated into a monastery by St. Feodosy (†1074). Feodosy, in fact, is considered the father of Russian monasticism. As abbot he saw to the strictest observance of the ascetic rules and made the Kiev cave monastery a model of its kind for the next two centuries. It has survived to the present day. The monks of the first generation carved their caves with their own hands into the soft stone of the riverbank. Besides the caves for dwelling places, other caves for burial were provided. In the course of centuries these catacombs grew to be many miles long, and the long generations of monks buried in them may still be seen there, since bodies in the caves do not decay—they mummify.

Founders' Monasteries

After Christianity had been made the state religion of the Duchy of Kiev by Prince (later St.) Vladimir, another type of monastic foundation arose. Under Prince Yaroslav (1019–54) a monastery of St. George and a convent of St. Irene were established in Kiev as founders' or princes' communities. This meant that the princes as founders held certain rights over these institutions, above all the right to appoint the abbots. They also supervised the administration of the monastic properties. Numerous foundations from before the Mongol invasions to the middle of the thirteenth century were of this type. In the establishment of these *ktitor* (= founder) monasteries we may see the direct influence of the Byzantine Church upon the princes

of Kiev: Theopempt of Kiev (c. 1039), the first metropolitan of the Byzantine hierarchy in the Duchy of Kiev,
was a Greek by birth. These founders' monasteries, together with the ecclesiastical hierarchy, formed the back-
bone of the evolving state church of the Kiev duchy.

The Struggle between Cenobitic and Skete Monasticism

The emergence of two different types of monastic institution on Russian soil affected the whole history of
Russia. As time went on and political conditions changed,
these two types of monasticism, so different in their internal
and external structures, were often pitted against each
other. The antagonism grew particularly bitter during the
fifteenth century. The two brands of monasticism differed
in their attitude toward the state, and toward the question
of monachal property. Skete monasticism, so christened
from the Greek word for eremitism, was responsible for
the great missionary work of the Russian monks in northern
Russia and Siberia—work we shall later examine in some
detail. The skete monks turned away from politics; they
were preachers of love and gentleness. As such they naturally opposed the injustice of princes and of the ecclesiastical hierarchies as well. Above all they denounced the cruel
methods that the ecclesiastical authorities were beginning
to apply to heretics and schismatics.

The other type of monasticism, which continued the
tradition of founders' monasteries, ranged itself on the side
of the secular princes. Strictest discipline prevailed in these
monasteries. The monks sought to increase the wealth of
their foundations in order to feed the poor and to help the
population in times of famine. Such monastic social work
was vitally important to the Grand Duchy of Moscow.
Yossif of Volokalamsk (1439–1515), one of the outstanding disciples of the greatest Russian abbot, St. Sergei, set
the style for the whole of the Moscow hierarchy and for
monastic institutions throughout the duchy. His partiality
for strict discipline also colored his political viewpoint.

Yossif became the theological defender of tsarist autocracy and dedicated all his energies to strengthening Orthodox tsarism. He not only established the ideology of Russian ecclesiastical statism but also was responsible for Orthodoxy's unbending harshness toward heretics and schismatics. During the last years of the reign of Ivan III (1462–1505) he personally persuaded the grand duke to undertake harsh punitive measures against heretics.

At the beginning of the sixteenth century the two monastic movements came to a direct clash. The Yossifites, as the advocates of an established church and tsarist autocracy were called, began to persecute the skete monks who lived in the lands beyond the Volga. At first the struggle revolved around the question of monastic property; after the 1550s it centered around the treatment of heretics. The monks beyond the Volga were consistently opposed to any use of force by the Church. They gave refuge to heretics persecuted by state and Church, and were therefore accused by the Yossifites of being themselves heretics. Finally their monasteries were dissolved and the monks themselves thrown into prison. The whole skete movement was annihilated. From that time on the triumphant Yossifites wielded the dominant influence in the Church of Muscovy. Their victory was inevitable for their aims accorded with the political aims of Moscow, whereas the skete monks had given government circles a wide berth. They would leave their hermitages to perform charitable services, but they never went to the palaces of the nobility or to Moscow itself. Like Gennady (†1565), the builder of the monasteries of Kostroma and Lyubimograd, they had loved to talk with peasants and stay in peasant huts where they could carry out their pastoral duties among the common people.

The dissolution of skete monasticism was a severe blow to the religious life of Russia. The tension between a free, charismatic, missionary-minded monasticism on the one hand and an authoritarian, statist monasticism on the other had proved an enormous spur to religious life in the Duchy of Kiev and later in Muscovy. Now that tension was gone; the state-church party had won a total victory. Thereafter the libertarian ideas that had been the property of eremitism were never allowed to gain foothold in Russia. Thus the dissolution of skete monasticism was the prelude to the subsequent tragedy: that Russia was left totally at the mercy of an intellectually paralyzed statist ecclesiasticism. The state asserted its supremacy in a series of repressive acts. Peter the Great eliminated the patriarchate; Empress Anna Ivanovna cruelly persecuted the monks; the ukase of 1764 closed more than half of all the monasteries in Russia. During these dark times the forbidden original spiritual impulses of Russian Christianity forced their way to the surface only within staretsism (see p. 99).

7. ORTHODOX MONASTICISM TODAY

Principal Types

Present-day Orthodox monasticism displays great uniformity of underlying ideas. True, every monastery has its own statutes, but their rules derive from the monastic rules of St. Basil, St. Sabas, St. Athanasius of Athos, and St. Theodore of Studion and are thus basically similar. The majority of present-day Orthodox monasteries are still of the old-type cenobitic pattern, in which all the monks lead their common life under the direction of a hegumen or abbot. Services, meals and work are shared. The monks sleep in common dormitories. The hegumen is elected by the monks and must be confirmed by the diocesan bishop or the patriarch. The monks of the cenoby are obliged to obey the hegumen unconditionally. Private property is forbidden.

In some monasteries, however, complete sharing of a common life has been partly or wholly abandoned. As long ago as the reign of Justinian, some monks in cenobitic monasteries were allowed to live as anchorites in special rooms. The impulse toward a more individual form of sanctity led, toward the end of the fourteenth century, to the special "idiorrhythmic" type of monasticism.[2] The purpose of this was to maintain the monachal framework and yet to permit the freedom and independence of the strictest type of sanctity, that of the anchorite. As it turned out, this variation in the pattern of cenobitic monasticism led to a loosening of the latter's austere discipline.

The tie between idiorrhythmic monasticism and old anchoritism is obvious. The monks subscribing to this rule live in small colonies of sketes or huts, as did the early Christian monastic colonies. The custom is for groups of three monks—a "family"—to live together in a single hut. Devotions are performed in the chapels of the separate huts. The monks of different sketes meet in the village church of the monastic settlement only on Sundays and holidays.

Alongside this practice, the pure type of anchoritism has survived to this day. The eremite lives in a hut near the monastery that supplies him with his food, or in a hermitage in some inaccessible place in the wilderness, or on a rocky cliff. There are still such eremites today on Athos, especially in the cliffs of the eastern peak of Mount Athos. The terrain here is so precipitous that the anchorites' huts often can be reached only by rope ladders.

Asceticism

A great many specifically Oriental characteristics of asceticism, reminiscent of Hindu or Buddhist ascetic practices, have lingered on in Orthodox monasticism. The stylite saints of Syrian monasticism, for example, can be traced to such non-Christian traditions. The anchorite established himself upon the capital of a solitary pillar, usually the remnant of some ancient temple, and remained there in a state of "eternal prayer." The fact that he never ceased meditating was expressed in his physical posture also. The ascetic assumed an attitude of prayer and remained so still

[2] Idiorrhythmic (Gk.) = living according to their own rhythm.

that ultimately—at least according to the legends—several Syrian saints had birds nesting upon their heads or upon their outstretched hands.

In Russia other saints won fame for extreme physical penances: fasts of up to forty days, prostrations repeated thousands of times—the penitent throwing himself down with arms outstretched and beating his forehead against the ground—attaching massive iron chains to themselves or wearing heavy metal crosses studded with sharp points against their bare skins, under their habits. Such instruments of castigation are still to be seen in the museums of Orthodox monasteries.

A certain relaxation of the austerity of cenobitic monasticism was introduced in the eighth century, with the distinction between the "micromorphic" and "macromorphic" monks. "Micromorphism" was introduced as a form of postulancy. By the vow of "macromorphism" the monk takes upon himself the full austerity of monastic life. A lesser degree of sanctity is required of the micromorphs. Acceptance into the rank of macromorph is marked by a special liturgical act, in which the stricter vows are pronounced. As a rule this is done only after the monk has undergone monastic life for many years in the rank of micromorph.

Attitude toward Learning

Orthodox monasteries have never become centers of learning in the same sense as the Roman Catholic monastic orders. This is due to the fact, already noted, that the Eastern monks dedicated themselves entirely to liturgy, mysticism and contemplation. Their fundamental attitude of withdrawal from "the world" led to their turning their backs on all forms of secular knowledge. Learning was regarded as an inducement to vanity and pride; for the holy man, it was better to steep oneself in the "folly" of the gospel. Whereas Western monasticism, especially the more recent orders, has contributed greatly to many fields of scholarly endeavor and monasteries today have become centers of historical research, the only branch of knowledge that has developed in the Orthodox monasteries has been the study of mystical theology and liturgics. Even in these fields the spirit of scholarship has more and more faded since the apogee of Byzantium. There have been some exceptions, to be sure: personalities like Maxim Grek (†1556), a celebrated Greek theologian and monk of Athos who was sent as a delegate to the court of the Russian tsar and was then kept in Moscow against his will. But his efforts to lend new impetus to theological studies had only limited success. On the whole the Orthodox monasteries have remained places for liturgical and meditative devotions. When at the beginning of the nineteenth century the Greek theologian Eugenios Bulgaris (1716–1806) attempted to found a theological academy on Athos, he met with furious resistance from the monks. The ruins of the great academy building remain there to this day, a monument to a lost cause, for the monks set it on fire.

8. RUSSIAN STARETSISM

But if Orthodox monasticism contributed little to the advancement of knowledge, it played a great part in the spiritual education of the people in another sphere. This sphere was pastoral care, the "cure of souls." Especially within Russia the example of the monks was a living force for piety. Orthodox Russian cenobitic monasteries permit monks of proven virtue to leave the community and live as anchorites in the vicinity of the monastery. The Russian name for such anchorites is *staretsy,* meaning those who build their cells in the woods. Throughout the centuries outstanding Russian *staretsy* have been the spiritual guides of princes and tsars, of philosophers and writers. They have also had a great effect upon the ordinary people of all classes.

9. MONASTICISM AND MYSTICISM

The monastic orders were the cradle of the most important spiritual force in Orthodoxy, mysticism. Its fundament was radical asceticism. As we have seen, the primitive Church's ascetic traditions, woven of elements taken from the Gospels and from Neoplatonism, have remained almost unaltered down to the present day. In the early days of the Church, however, asceticism was more strongly influenced by expectation of the impending end of the world and the dawn of the kingdom of heaven. Ascetics prepared for the coming of the kingdom by vanquishing what was worldly in themselves. The basis of later monastic asceticism was not so much the eschatological principle as Neoplatonic dualism. The monk's task was to devote himself wholly to God in mystic contemplation and to withdraw as far as possible from all involvement in the things of the flesh and of this world. This total devotion to God was so radical and exclusive that ultimately it took precedence over one's obligations to one's fellowmen. The highest form of asceticism was supposed to be complete liberation from the world, solitude in which the pious monk's entire moral and intellectual energies were directed toward God. The conditions of the monastery were intended to further the prayer and contemplation that were the monk's principal task.

The monastic state, therefore, is still referred to as the state of "angelic life." Similarly the habit worn by the monk is referred to as the angel's robe. The ascetic who frees himself from all temptations of this world feels that right here on earth he is concentrating his efforts upon the kingdom of heaven. His aim is to achieve union with the celestial world in this life. This union takes place by way of Christ, the divine Logos, who has descended to earth and opened the way for men to become divine themselves.

However, the monk's mystical experience, in which he participates in union with the transcendental world, is not restricted to the level of "Christ mysticism," that is to say, becoming one with Christ. It rises to "God mysticism," in which the monk, through experiencing union with Christ, the Image of the Father, achieves a vision of the divine Light Itself. The most sublime expression of this monastic mysticism was the doctrine of *hesychasm*,[3] which was most assiduously cultivated on Athos in the fourteenth century. The peak mystical experience of the hesychastic monks is vision of the divine Light which comes as the reward of methodically practiced contemplation.

This ascetic monastic mysticism was celebrated in the poems of the great Byzantine hymnists, above all those of Simeon the New Theologian (c. 960–c. 1036). Such mystical hymnody has been kept alive in the Orthodox Church down to the present time by being incorporated into the liturgy and thus presented to churchgoers of every parish in daily or Sunday prayers and hymns. The principles of self-abnegation are spelled out in the liturgy of consecration of a monk. After the abbot has put numerous traditional questions to the novice, he addresses him with the following formula: "If you now wish to become a monk, purify yourself above all things of every taint of the flesh and the spirit and acquire holiness in the fear of God. Work, wear yourself out, in order to acquire humility, whereby you will become the heir of everlasting goods. Put off pride and the shamelessness of worldly habits. Practice obedience toward all. Perform the duties that are imposed upon you without complaint. Be enduring in prayer. Be neither lazy nor sleepy during the vigils. Steadfastly resist temptations. Be not neglectful of your fasts, but know that prayer and fasting are the way to win favor with God. . . . Henceforth nothing must matter to you but God. You shall love neither father nor mother nor brothers, nor any in your family. You shall not love yourself more than God. . . . Nothing shall restrain you from following

---

[3] From *hesuchia* (Gk.) = tranquillity.

Christ. . . . You will have to suffer, you will go hungry, you will endure thirst, you will be robbed of your clothing, you will suffer injustice, you will be mocked, you will be persecuted, you will be slandered, you will be visited by many bitter tribulations—all these sufferings are the token of a life in keeping with the will of God."

Naturally, ideal and reality are often at odds. But even in times of decadence Eastern monasticism has repeatedly attained great heights. It is not out of the question that the present era of an apparently total decay of Orthodox monasticism will be followed by an age of renewal and practical realization of a time-honored ideal.

VII.

Missionary Work and the Spread
of the Orthodox Church

1. DID ORTHODOXY FAIL
AS A MISSION CHURCH?

The Eastern Church has often been charged with failure in its missionary work. Prejudiced observers have contended that it felt little impulse to convert the non-Christian peoples living in its midst or at its borders, that it was satisfied with preserving the status quo and preferred to keep its dogmas and liturgies to itself. A prejudiced opinion of this kind is largely due to ignorance, in western Europe, of the actual missionary work carried out by the Eastern Orthodox Church. It is also, perhaps, based upon the situation of the Orthodox remnants who found themselves engulfed by the triumphant sweep of Islam in the Near East and central Asia.

It is true that the tiny colonies of Orthodoxy in Syria, Lebanon, Palestine, Egypt and Ethiopia, as well as the Orthodox Thomaeans in India, and the battered Nestorian Church in Persia, display little missionary activity today. During the first spread of Islam, during the time of the Mongol hordes in the thirteenth and fourteenth centuries, and again since the establishment of Turkish rule, these churches were subject to such violent persecution that the once flourishing Christian communities were almost wiped out. The Muhammadan authorities have forbidden the survivors to undertake any missionary work among Muslims. Islamic law, moreover, provides the severest penalties for the conversion of Muslims to Christianity. The Indian Thomaean Christians have become, under the influence of Hindu ideas of caste, a closed caste and have thus forfeited all missionary aspirations. Centuries of political repression of the Orthodox and schismatic churches in the Near and Far East snuffed out whatever missionary zeal might have been felt by those beleaguered Christians.

Even when times changed and repression was lifted, these churches were no longer capable of recovering their militancy. During the period of European colonial expansion Britain and France in particular wrote clauses concerning missions into their international treaties. Thus Roman Catholic and Protestant missions were able to begin their operations in the Near East under the most favorable terms. The contiguity of active Roman Catholic and Protestant missions in the Near East, alongside the old Christian churches whose character was stamped by centuries of passivity, greatly contributed to this notion that Orthodoxy is incapable of missionary work.

2. THE MISSIONARY METHODS OF THE BYZANTINE CHURCH

It is, however, altogether wrong to conclude, from instances of this sort, that the Eastern Orthodox Church has completely lacked the missionary spirit from the beginning. In fact, Orthodoxy engaged in the most vigorous missionary work during the period of its own most vital growth. By the third and fourth centuries it had penetrated eastward as far as Persia and India, and from those countries, in its Nestorian variety, to China, central Asia and Mongolia. It was also expanding westward; the Germanic tribes migrating through western Europe were first Christianized by missionaries from Asia Minor and Byzantium. The Byzantine Church also sent its missionaries to the north, northeast and northwest; West, South and East Slavs were converted by them. Much of this missionary activity was subsequently forgotten by the West because Roman Catholics later replaced the Orthodox missionaries, especially in Moravia, and incorporated the Germanic and West Slavic tribes into the community of the Roman Catholic Church. In its time, however, the missionary work of the Orthodox Church was a tremendous achievement, and its aftereffects survived for centuries, though overlaid by later Roman Catholic work among the heathen. We shall deal with the missionary activity and spread of the Orthodox Church in some detail for the very reason that it has been so largely ignored by the West.

3. MISSION AND NATIONALITY

In its most flourishing period the Orthodox Church not only poured much of its spiritual dynamism into spreading the gospel among non-Christian peoples, but did so in consonance with a theological principle that distinctly furthered the success of this missionary work. The principle was: to preach to the various peoples in their own language, and to employ the ordinary tongue of the people in the liturgy for divine services. In the Syrian Church, Syrian; in the Armenian Church, Armenian; in the Coptic Church, Coptic; in the Georgian Church, Georgian; these were the languages of sermon, hymn and liturgy.

Behind this practice lay a specific theological view of the vernacular. The primitive Church had consulted the Bible and drawn from it certain conclusions concerning man's linguistic evolution. Thus, the early theologians set up two parallel events: one was the story of the confusion of tongues at the Tower of Babel, and the other the story of the Pentecostal outpouring of the Spirit with its accompanying miracle of "speaking in tongues." These were regarded as key points in the history of redemption. The confusion of tongues at Babel (Genesis 11) was seen as punishment for man's defiance of God. The many languages thus engendered destroyed the unity of true knowledge of God and promoted the spread of false religions, so that each people created its own gods. The "miracle of tongues," on the other hand, was a token of God's mercy and his desire to redeem all nations. The Pentecostal miracle was considered to be the baptism of the vernacular tongues; henceforth the vernacular was exalted into an instrument for annunciation of the divine message of redemption throughout the world, among all peoples.

These concepts are still impressed upon the Orthodox believer, for they are incorporated into the liturgy:

"With the tongues of foreign peoples hast Thou, Christ, renewed Thy disciples, that they might thereby be heralds of God, of the immortal Word that vouchsafes to our souls the great mercy. . . . Upon a time the tongues were confounded by reason of the Tower's blasphemy. But now tongues are filled with wisdom by reason of the glory of knowledge of God. Then God condemned the blasphemers by sin; now Christ has illuminated the fishermen by the Spirit. Then the garbling of language was imposed for punishment; now the harmony of languages is renewed for the salvation of our souls. . . . The power of the divine Spirit has solemnly united into one the divided voices of those who agreed ill in their thoughts, has joined them in concord by giving to the believers insight into knowledge of the Threeness in which we were confirmed. . . . When, descending, He confused the languages, the All-highest divided the peoples. When He sent out the tongues of fire, He called all to oneness. And in concord hymn we the All-holy Spirit."

Since this was their belief, Orthodox missionaries of all countries and all epochs made a point of casting both gospel and liturgy into the vernacular of the peoples of their mission. Thus it was that the Orthodox missions in both West and East, in the Germanic, Slavic and Asiatic lands, had an enormously creative influence upon the development of the vulgar tongues. Many of the languages of Europe, the Near East, Siberia and central Asia were raised to the rank of literary languages by the work of the Orthodox missionaries in translating the Bible and liturgical writings.

Nowadays few people realize the significance of such translations. Translating the Bible into a vernacular means enlisting that language for the work of building the kingdom of God. The language is used to build the spiritual edifice, and lines are laid down governing its further literary development. Such a translation brings about both the rebirth and baptism of a language. The translator of the Bible is confronted with the creative task of expressing, with the often inadequate means of a hitherto nonliterary vernacular, the immense body of spiritual and earthly, natural and social, sacred and profane ideas that are contained in the books of the Old and New Testaments. To perform such translation means, in fact, to conquer for the first time the intellectual and natural universe for the language in question, and therefore for the people who speak that language.

4. THE MISSION AMONG THE TEUTONS

Beginnings of the Teutonic Mission

The Orthodox missionary work among the Germanic peoples has been largely forgotten. Yet the first important Teutonic state and the first Teutonic culture to emerge from the *Völkerwanderung*—the kingdom of Theodoric the Great—was largely shaped by Byzantine elements. Carried along by the advancing wave of Goths, the missionary work of the Orthodox Church extended far to the West.

The eastern Teutons had started their migrations from what would seem to have been their original tribal homes in Sweden. Prevented by other Germanic tribes from moving westward during the third and fourth centuries, they had violently broken through to the south and southeast and had poured into the Roman Empire in two great streams: the Goths by crossing the lower reaches of the Danube; the Vandals, Alans and Suevi, with the Burgundians following somewhat later, by crossing the Rhine. All these Germanic tribes were Christianized in somewhat the same manner as the East Gothic tribes, who had come under the influence of Orthodox Christendom. These East Goths, or Ostrogoths, controlled the region stretching from the Vistula to the lower Volga and the Crimea.

Christianity apparently took hold among the Goths first in the region bordering the Black Sea. A bishop from Gothia appeared at the Council of Nicaea in 325, and the term "Diocese of Gothia" can be traced in the Crimea until as late as the tenth century. These Goths had been converted by priests and monks of the Byzantine Church. Missionary work among the Goths on the Danube likewise went forward during the third and fourth centuries, in part carried on by prisoners of war whom the Goths had captured during their raiding expeditions into Byzantine territory. Among the Fathers of the Church, Basil the Great took a particular interest in the Gothic Church, which he regarded as an offshoot of the Cappadocian Church. Around the middle of the fourth century a campaign of violent repression was launched against the Christian Goths by the Gothic king Athanaric (†381), a persecution that resulted in numerous martyrs. Groups of Christian Goths fled from their own lands into Byzantine territory, settling in Thrace. At the beginning of the fifth century Patriarch John Chrysostom (c. 347–407) provided the Goths in Constantinople with a church of their own in which services were held in the Gothic language.

Teutonic Arianism

The most important missionary work among the Goths was undertaken by the Arian Church of Asia Minor. The founder of that offshoot of Orthodoxy was one Arius, a presbyter of Alexandria (†336), whose interpretation of the nature of the Logos and of the relationship between the Son of God and the Father was later condemned as heretical by the Byzantine Church. But the newly converted Goths were scarcely conscious of Arius' special Christology and of the subtleties of his theological speculations. They were called Arians simply because at the time of their conversion Arianism was the dominant doctrine in the Church of the Empire. They remained Arians after a shift in ecclesiastical politics resulted in the condemnation of Arianism as a heresy.

Wulfila

Bishop Wulfila (Ulfilas) (c. 311–83) was responsible for the religious, liturgical and constitutional character of Gothic Arianism. Wulfila's grandparents had been Christians from Cappadocia in Asia Minor who were captured by the Goths in 264 and held prisoner. As the son of a Gothic father and Cappadocian mother, Wulfila commanded the Greek, Latin and Gothic languages. In his twenties he was sent to Constantinople as a member of a Gothic embassy. As emissaries of a group that had heroically withstood severe persecutions, he and his coreligionists were well received by the Emperor Constantius II. Wulfila received theological training in Asia Minor, and at the age of thirty was consecrated by Eusebius of Nicomedia as "Bishop of those of the Christian faith, living in the Gothic land." He returned to his homeland and continued his work among Christian and pagan Goths for thirty-three years.

The success of Wulfila's missionary work was due above all to his translation of the Bible into Gothic. This alone made it possible for the Gothic tribes to assimilate Christianity. Through this translation, moreover, Wulfila enormously extended the linguistic horizon of one Germanic people. He transformed the hitherto unwritten vernacular of the West Goths into a literary language that could be used for the dissemination of the new universal religion.

The Arianism of the Germanic tribes vanished completely after a few centuries—only a few churches in Ravenna and on the Iberian Peninsula still bear witness to its onetime sway over much of Europe. But the German language still bears the marks of Wulfila's mighty literary achievement. The German words for God, devil, angel, church, bishop, penance, transgression, faith, and so on, were created by Wulfila, either taken from the native Gothic word-stock and given Christian meanings, or introduced directly from the Greek into Gothic, whence they found their way into German. Thus the spirit that a disciple of Near Eastern theology breathed into his translation of the Bible still affects the language and literature of the German people.

5. THE MISSION
TO THE SLAVS OF CYRIL AND METHODIUS

The second westward missionary thrust of the Byzantine Church was led by the "apostles of the Slavs," Cyril (†869) and Methodius (†885), who went first to the West Slavs, especially in the Moravian kingdom, and afterwards to the South Slavic tribes, the Bulgarians, Serbs and Dalmatians.

Methodius and Constantine (for that was Cyril's real name) were brothers, Greeks from Salonika, who knew the Bulgarian-Macedonian dialect spoken in the Slavic settlements around their native city. Constantine was carefully educated in Constantinople. He early turned to missionary work and first went out among the Muhammadans, then to the kingdom of the Khazars on the shores of the Sea of Azov. Shortly before his death he became a monk and adopted the name of Cyril. His brother Methodius spent the early part of his life as a government administrator in the Slavic territories of the Byzantine Empire. He likewise became a monk and abbot of the famous monastery of Polychron.

Rastislav, Duke of Moravia (846–70) had established an independent West Slavic kingdom. In order to maintain his autonomy, he wanted to make the Moravian Church independent of the Frankish Church. He expelled the German priests and appealed to the emperor at Constantinople, Michael III, to send teachers for his people. Constantine and Methodius were chosen for this task. They arrived in Moravia in 864 and devoted themselves chiefly to teaching, in order to supply the Moravian Church with native Slavic priests. While in Moravia, Constantine translated parts of the Scriptures and the liturgy into the Slavic language. He is probably responsible for the creation of the oldest Slavic alphabet, the "Glagolitic" script; documents written in that script go back as far as the ninth century.

Members of the Orthodox Church were at this time not conscious of any deep separation from the Church of Rome; in fact, the prestige of the two brothers in Moravia rested upon their feat of having brought the relics of Bishop Clement of Rome to Moravia from the Crimea—according to legend Clement had been exiled to the Crimea during the persecutions and had died there.

In keeping with this spirit the two brothers, although sent out by the Byzantine patriarch, hoped to have the Roman pope endorse their founding of a Slavic-speaking church in Moravia. A decree from Rome, they thought, would still the hostility of the Frankish clergy. Consequently, after laboring in Moravia for three and a half years, they made their way across Pannonia to Rome, where they were given a ceremonious reception by Pope Hadrian II. Constantine died in Rome on February 14, 869, and was buried in the Church of St. Clement. Methodius, after being consecrated archbishop and appointed papal legate to Pannonia and

Moravia, was given an organizational and missionary assignment among the Slavs similar to that which Boniface had received for the German tribes a century and a half earlier. But because of the war then being fought between the Moravian and German dukes, Methodius remained in Pannonian territory, which had hitherto been the missionary zone of the Archbishop of Salzburg, who greatly objected to this intrusion. This was the beginning of a long series of disputes, in the course of which a Bavarian synod condemned Methodius and had him imprisoned for two and a half years. The central issue was the German clergy's opposition to the introduction of Slavic liturgy and the establishment of a Slavic ecclesiastical province with Slavic as the official language of the churches. Finally the heads of the German churches succeeded in persuading the Pope to oppose Hadrian's original plan. Pope Stephen VI forbade the use of Slavic in the Church. The pupils of Methodius were expelled from their posts. The newly established hierarchy was nearly wiped out by the Hungarian invasions after 900; in 950 Moravia was assigned to the diocese of Regensburg, and in 973 to Prague. This completed the destruction of what had been the essence of Cyril and Methodius' lifework. The West Slavic tribes remained for the time being under the guidance of the German Church. In Poland, too, the Latin rite became established. The attempt to set up a West Slavic Church under the sovereignty of Rome, but with Slavic as the official language, had failed.

Nevertheless, some part of the work of the two brothers was unexpectedly saved. After their expulsion from Moravia the pupils of Methodius continued their work among the South Slavic tribes along the Danube and in the Balkans. In Bulgaria they set up a Slavic Church, no longer under the dominion of Rome since Rome had ruled against tolerating the Slavic ritual, but under the protection of the Byzantine Church which still subscribed to its old missionary principle of permitting each nation to conduct the liturgy in its own language.

Although the work of the "apostles of the Slavs" in the Moravian kingdom was not successful and was ultimately rejected by Rome, their literary achievements were of tremendous importance for future missions. Cyril became the creator of the Old Church Slavonic language by translating the Bible and liturgy into his native Bulgarian-Macedonian dialect. Many historical and philological problems connected with his work are still unsolved or the subject of much contention. But the fact remains that he laid the groundwork for a Slavic ecclesiastical literature on which later missions among the East Slavs could build.

6. THE MISSION AMONG THE EAST SLAVS

The Mission in Northeastern Russia

By the end of the eleventh century the territory of the East Slavs had been Christianized, though not completely so, from Novgorod in the north to beyond Kiev in the south—what the Russians called "the land along the road from the Varangians to the Greeks." The princes of Rus, as the Duchy of Kiev was called, had actively encouraged this movement. The populations of other racial stock in the area had been only sketchily won for Christianity. This was true, for example, of the territory around Rostov, on the upper reaches of the Volga, known to Russian traders as the "way to the Saracens." The direction of future Christian expansion was decided by political conditions; it had to be toward the northeast. The division of the land under the sons of Yaroslav (1019–54) led to a waning of the power of Kiev; the center of power shifted toward the north. The Polovtsians, pressing against the southern border of the steppes, were more than a match for the Russian princes, even when the latter met them with their combined forces. The second half of the eleventh and almost the entire twelfth centuries were filled with these struggles. The population of the southern parts of Rus left their homes

in despair and sought a new and more peaceful life farther
to the north, "beyond the forests."

This displacement of the center of power toward the
north was decisively influenced by the Crusades, which
changed the whole nature of trade and economic life in
the Orient. The newly opened Levantine trade on the Mediterranean dealt a deathblow to commerce on the longer
road "from the Varangians to the Greeks," and also put ˊ
a stop to the clumsy and difficult caravan traffic from central Europe to the Orient. Kiev, hitherto the center of
European commerce between North and South and West
and East, became unimportant. Novgorod, on the other
hand, developed into an important transshipment site and
the link between the West and the Russian East. The hinter-
land of Novgorod was more thickly settled. In Vladimir-
on-the-Klyazma a new political center arose, whose heritage was later taken over by Moscow.

Mission and Colonization in Northeastern Russia

Russian missionary work went hand in hand with Russian colonization. The early colonization was by no means
a military conquest. It was a matter of peaceful but continuous infiltration which resulted in a fraternal mingling
of new settlers and the native population rather than suppression of the latter by the former. The history of the
colonization of northern Russia as far as Arkhangelsk to
the north and along the Volga and Kama to the Urals in
the east is a story of slow, peaceful expansion, with hunters,
traders and monks leading the way, penetrating ever deeper
into the northeastern forests, and gradually followed by
peasant settlers who cleared the land. Religious penetration
of these areas accompanied the colonization. The Orthodox
religion of the Russian settlers became established not only
as a set of religious ideas, but also as a way of life. The
calendar and the customs of the Orthodox Church operated
as a cultural and civilizing force. The Mongol invasions of
eastern Europe interrupted this development, but on the

other hand, the menace of the Mongols gave greater urgency to the need to colonize and carry on missionary work.

7. MISSION AND SPREAD
OF THE RUSSIAN ORTHODOX CHURCH

Missionary Work before the Tatar Invasion

Russian monks on missions had partly followed, partly preceded the Russian colonizers in the northeast some time before the Tatar hordes swept across the steppes. Throughout this period in which Christianity was taking hold "wherever scythe and ax were swung," missionary activity was in the hands of individual monks exclusively. By the twelfth century, Christianity had penetrated into the region of Vyatka, west of Perm; from 1159 on, the monk Avraamy spread the gospel among the Votyaks and Cheremisses there. Yet up to the beginning of the thirteenth century, Russian monasteries were to be found only within the territory of cities; the monasteries were "satellites," not advance posts and disseminators of Christian life.

After the Tatar Invasion

This situation changed completely after the Mongols came. The first Mongol incursion into Russia (1222–23) was followed by an almost immediate withdrawal of the invaders to central Asia. But after the death of Genghis Khan (1227), his grandson Batu settled permanently along the lower Volga with his horde. From this center his mounted bands struck up river in 1238, taking by storm all the cities that lay in their path. Only Novgorod was not conquered, thanks to a thaw that forced the Mongols to turn back. In 1240 Batu turned westward. His Mongols captured and plundered Kiev, poured over southern Europe as far as the Adriatic Sea and invaded upper Italy. Hearing that Ogadai, the Great Khan, had just died, Batu did not exploit his victory over the Christian armies of the West at Liegnitz in 1241; he returned to the lower Volga and there set up the "Kingdom of the Golden Horde" of Kipchak, with Sarai on the river Akhtuba as its capital. Henceforth the Russian princes had to pay homage to their new masters there and in far Karakorum, the residence of the Great Khan. Russia had become a province of the Tatar Empire.

The Anchorite Movement

The Mongol scourge produced a penitential mood in the Russian people, a state of mind which found expression in a strong anchorite movement. Many monasteries in the conquered cities were destroyed, many monks killed, and the survivors poured northward with the throngs of refugees. In these turbulent times the entire Russian people were gripped with a profound longing to escape from the world. Many simple folk resolved upon a monastic life in order to save their souls. Whereas previously the monks had followed the settlers, henceforth they preceded the settlers into the wilderness of the northern forests. The converse process now took place: the hermitages in the hitherto inaccessible wastelands attracted farmers, who settled in their vicinity, seeking simultaneously religious and economic support.

The monastic reform of St. Sergei of Radonesh (1314–93) stimulated still further monastic colonization and resulted in a network of monasteries scattered over the whole of north and northeast Russia. The Troitzkaya Laura in the forests northeast of Moscow became the starting point for the two main lines of future mission and colonization by monks. One of these lines ran along the Kostroma toward the Vychegda; the other followed the Zeksna to the White Lake (Beloye Ozero). The monasteries thus founded in the fourteenth century became the most important missionary centers for that era and for future centuries also. Thus, for example, there was the famous monastery of Valamo on a group of islands in Lake Ladoga, founded in

1329 by the monks Sergei and German. It subsequently became the center for missionary work among the East Karelians. The mission to the Lapps was centered in the monastery founded by Lazar (†1391), a monk born in Constantinople, upon the island of Murmansk in Lake Onega. Among the many daughter monasteries of the Troitzkaya Laura, the most prominent were the monastery of St. Cyril (named after its founder) and that of Ferapontov, a friend of the saint, which was established nearby in 1397–98. During the following century the monks of the Belozersk group founded no less than nineteen additional monasteries, including (in 1426) the noted one on Solovetski Island in the White Sea, which was to achieve a terrible notoriety in the Soviet Union as a place of banishment.

8. THE POSITION OF THE RUSSIAN ORTHODOX CHURCH IN THE TIME OF THE MONGOLS

Russia between Rome and the Mongols

After the Mongols had subjugated the Russian principalities, the Russian Church was accorded the protection of Mongol religious laws. These were set forth in the code known as the Great Yasa. Thus both the organization and the property of the Russian Church remained inviolate. Russia under Mongol dominance became more alienated than before from the Catholic West. The existing strains and antagonisms between the churches of East and West were deepened. It might be thought that under the pressure of Mongol occupation the Russian Church would have turned toward the Roman Catholic West, hoping and appealing for liberation from the Mongol yoke, even at the price of ecclesiastical subordination to Rome. But in fact only a single Russian prince took this course—Prince Daniel of Galicia, the westernmost Russian principality which had long been strongly influenced by Roman Catholicism.

Prince Daniel entered into negotiations with the Pope and in 1253 received the insignia of royalty from him.

Estrangement from Rome. Prince Alexander Nevsky

Meanwhile the Pope's efforts to summon the Catholic powers to a crusade against the Mongols bore no fruit. Cyril, the west Russian monk who at the instigation of Prince Daniel had been elected metropolitan of Kiev, took offense at Daniel's negotiations with the Curia and switched his allegiance to Prince Alexander, the nominal ruler of Kiev, who actually resided in Novgorod. Alexander made the fateful decision that separated Russia from the Catholic West. To him the Roman Catholic Church meant the Teutonic Order of Knights, which was waging its crusades not only against the pagan peoples of the Baltic region, but also against the west Russian principalities—and that at a moment of crisis for the Mongol Empire.

The crisis took the following form.

In the year 1251, Mangu began his rule as Great Khan of the Mongol Empire. The Kingdom of the Golden Horde, dominated by Batu since 1242, became relatively independent under Mangu. The new Great Khan confirmed Batu in his rule and entrusted him with supervision of the Russian princes. Batu in turn delegated the administration of Russian affairs to his son and co-ruler, Sartak. Sartak, however, was a Nestorian Christian. Prince Alexander, facing the dual threat of crusading Roman Catholic Teutonic Knights who were attacking his country from the west, and Mongolian khans who dominated it from the east, decided in favor of an alliance with the Mongols. It is significant that the Russian people have made this militant prince, who defeated the Teutonic Knights on the ice of the Neva and who remained a faithful ally and subject of the Mongol ruler, their greatest national hero. Undoubtedly Alexander's decision was influenced by the fact that the enemies from the West were of the Latin faith, while the Mongol Khan was a Nestorian Christian and as such followed a religion closer to his own than Roman Catholicism. In deciding against the West, Alexander could count on the full sympathy of the clergy of his country. When he returned from Sarai confirmed by the khan as Prince of Vladimir, he was solemnly hailed upon his arrival in Vladimir by the Metropolitan Cyril, the clergy and the whole people.

There was no change in the situation under Batu's son and successor, Sartak; in fact, the ties with the Mongols were strengthened since relations between the Mongol khanate and the Byzantine Empire had entered a new phase. During the period of Latin rule in Byzantium (1204–61) the exiled Greek emperors in Nicaea maintained friendly ties with the ilkhans in Persia. After the restoration of the Greek Empire, Emperor Michael VIII set about establishing amicable relations with the khans of the Kipchak Mongols, the rulers of the Golden Horde. The consequence was the opening of a new trade route between Kipchak and Egypt by way of Byzantium.

The Condition of the Russian Church under the Mongols

Religious life in the Mongol Empire was governed by the Great Yasa, the rule that Persian and Arabic historians of the fourteenth century considered to be of divine origin. One of the tenets of the Yasa is that of tolerance toward all religions in the Mongol Empire. "Since Genghis Khan belonged to no religion, he preferred none above any other; on the contrary, he was wont to show respect to venerated wise men and hermits of all peoples, regarding such conduct as a way to please God. He commanded his people to do likewise." He was not indifferent in matters of faith. Rather, he considered it his duty to establish order and peace in religion as he believed he was doing on the temporal plane—had not Heaven itself assigned him the task of pacifying the whole world? The Great Yasa did not tamper with the laws of any given religion but set up a system within which the various religions as well as the various peoples could live peacefully side by side. The Mongol Empire actually fostered a kind of ecumene of world religions. Under its protection the Christian Church, including the Nestorian Church and—from the thirteenth century on—the new Roman Catholic missions, could function and develop in relative freedom.

This situation was somewhat changed when the khans were converted to Muhammedanism. But it is noteworthy that even after the dramatic conversion of the khan of the Golden Horde, the fundamental principle of toleration of all religions was not abandoned in the Russian principalities. The Mongols continued to observe the tenets of the Great Yasa in their relations toward the Orthodox Church. Priests and monks of all religions, as well as physicians and scholars, were tax-free and exempt from military service. The Great Yasa guaranteed the same freedoms to Buddhist priests of China as it did to priests and monks in Persia and Russia. Under shelter of this fundamental law the clergy and laity of all faiths and churches lived peacefully side by side from Peking to Karakorum.

Collapse of the Union with Rome

By this time so strong a sense of independence had grown up in Russia that Michael VIII's policy of union with Rome, which he had launched at the second Council of Lyon in 1274, encountered fierce resistance from the Russian clergy. On the other hand their relations with the Mongols were so warm that under Sartak's successor, Birkai, a Russian Orthodox diocese was set up in Sarai on the Volga, the capital of the Golden Horde. Under the new Great Khan, Mangu Timur, the Russian Church flourished. Ties between the Mongols and Byzantium likewise grew stronger, especially after 1273 when a marital alliance between the imperial house of the Palaeologi and the rulers of Kipchak was successfully arranged. Mangu Timur confirmed all the privileges of the Russian Church, clergy and monks which his predecessors had granted. In return the Russian clergy was expected to pray fervently and sincerely in their churches for Mangu Timur, his family and his successors.

Orthodox Mission among the Mongols

During this period the Russian Orthodox Church also proceeded to undertake missionary work among the Mongols themselves. In 1259 a prince of the Yukhides was converted to Christianity by Bishop Cyril of Rostov and baptized Pyotr; he was later canonized by the Orthodox Church as Pyotr Ordinsky—Peter of the Horde. Given the prevailing tolerance in the Mongol Empire, a prince could change his religion without stepping down from his station. Pyotr's presence in Rostov resulted in the strengthening of friendly relations between the dukes of Rostov and the khan, and ultimately to marital alliances. In 1257, Prince Gleb traveled into Mongolia and married a Mongol princess who accepted baptism and was given the Christian name of Theodora. The Orthodox bishops of Sarai, in addition to their work among Christians at the court of the khan of the Golden Horde, were also employed by the Mongol khans for diplomatic missions to the West, especially to Constantinople. The ties between Russian and Mongolian princely houses persisted, even after Islam spread not only to the ilkhans of Asia Minor but also to the Golden Horde. Under Khan Tuda Mangu, Grand Duke Fedor of Smolensk, formerly of Yaroslavl, enjoyed particularly high prestige. He spent several years at the Mongol court. After the death of his first wife, Princess Maria of Yaroslavl, he married a daughter of Mangu Timur, who was baptized and received the Christian name of Anna. Similarly, Prince Yuri of Moscow spent several years at the court of the Horde and married Uzbeg's sister Konchak, who was given the baptismal name of Agatha.

Missionary Work in Siberia and Alaska

To trace all the further history of Russian missionary work would carry us too far afield; Glazik's excellent book (see Bibliography) covers the field. In every century there have emerged from Russian missionary work impressive Christian personalities who have been unjustly overlooked or forgotten by Western church historians. In the fourteenth century there was Stefan of Perm, in the sixteenth St. Gury, in the seventeenth Bishop Filofey Lechinsky, the "beacon light of the Siberian peoples." We shall give a brief account of just one of these great missionaries, Innokenty Venyaminov (1797–1879), who in the nineteenth century carried the gospel of the Orthodox Church to Kamchatka, the Aleutians and to then Russian Alaska.

Innokenty, born in 1797 in a village of the Siberian province of Irkutsk, early proved to be a man of extraordinary versatility; he was artisan and artist, philologist and natural scientist, theologian, pastor and prince of the Church in one person. After his marriage in 1821 he was consecrated a priest and assigned to a church in Irkutsk. In 1823 he undertook missionary work in the Aleutians. He preached to the Aleuts in their native tongue and made a first translation into Aleut of the catechism, the historical books of the Bible, and various New Testament writings. In a relatively short time he succeeded in establishing a model Christian community among this hitherto neglected population. He visited one island after the other, and also made a journey to the American mainland, where he converted the pagan tribes of Alaska and "after suitable examination and admonition," baptized them.

Along with his missionary activity, Innokenty also devoted himself to geographical and linguistic studies of these territories. He wrote *Notes on the Islands of the District of Unalaska* and a grammar of Aleutian based on the dialect of the Fox Islands. In addition he was the author of a religious primer for his native Christians, *Guide to the Kingdom of Heaven*. This book, which sets forth in simple terms the fundamental truths of Orthodox Christianity, became exceedingly popular after it was published in 1841 in a Russian and an Old Church Slavonic translation. Later it was translated into many of the other languages of the Russian missionary churches; by 1881 it had appeared in twenty-two editions, including one in German which was used as a devotional manual in the German Protestant congregations of the Black Sea region.

After ten years of activity on Unalaska, the largest island of the Aleutians, Innokenty moved to Novo-Arkangelsk (now Sitka) on Baranof Island. Here, too, he prepared the first grammar of the Koluschan language in order to be able to preach the Christian gospel to the people in their own tongue. He then undertook the long journey to St. Petersburg to put the spiritual and material needs of his vast diocese before the Holy Synod and propose measures that would place the Orthodox Church upon a firmer footing and guarantee its further expansion in America. Returning to the Aleutians, he resumed his missionary work with renewed impetus and remarkable success. He continued his linguistic labors as well, translating for the Koluschans the evangelical and apostolic pericopes.[1] Under his supervision the mission on the American mainland also made great progress. From 1842 his missionaries worked in the river valley of the Kuskokwim, with Nushagak as their center, from 1845 in the Kenai Peninsula, and from Ikogmut up the Yukon. In 1859 he divided the American missionary territory from the Kamchatka eparchy, establishing it as the vicariate of Sitka and consecrating the previous rector of his native seminary, Archimandrite Pyotr, as first episcopal vicar.

The ·American mission was seriously hampered after 1867 by the sale of the Russian territories in America to the United States. Innokenty attempted to conserve as many gains for the faith as possible. He raised the vicariate of Sitka to the rank of an independent diocese. When in 1872 the bishop of this diocese abandoned his seat in Novo-Arkangelsk in order to devote himself principally to the

[1] Pericope (Gk. = extract), a passage of Scripture to be used in the liturgy and as text for the sermon on specific days.

Russian communities in California and Canada, the Orthodox cause in Alaska went into a decline. It was not until
1900 that Alaska, on the urging of the Orthodox Missionary Society in Moscow, was once more assigned its own
episcopal vicar.

In 1850 Innokenty, who had meanwhile launched a successful mission in Kamchatka, was appointed archbishop.
This promotion spurred his zeal still further. He traveled
to the extreme north of Siberia to extend his work to the
region around Anadyr. In 1852 he succeeded in transfer-
ring the whole province of Yakutsk to the diocese of Kamchatka, and moved his episcopal seat to Yakutsk. From this
new center the missionary work among the pagans of his
eparchy was extended and consolidated. In 1855 he undertook a new mission into the Amur territory. By the Treaty
of Aigun between Russia and China in 1858, Russia received the lands between Ussuri and the Sea of Japan. Innokenty thereupon moved to Blagoveshchensk on the Amur
and proceeded to reorganize the Church of eastern Siberia.
By this time he was nearly blind, his sight having been almost completely destroyed by long treks over the dazzling
snowfields of the north. Nevertheless, at the age of sixty-
three he traveled to Japan, at sixty-five to Kamchatka, and
at seventy into the interior of the Amur territory, forever
occupied with preaching and teaching, forever afire with
new missionary plans and new scholarly tasks.

The death of Filaret, the Metropolitan of Moscow, ushered in the last decisive change in his eventful life. Recognized by all as the most important personality in the Russian episcopate, Innokenty was elected Metropolitan of
Moscow at the age of seventy-one. Having attained the
highest office in the Russian Church, he was in a position
to entrust his missionary schemes to a permanent organization. He founded the Orthodox Missionary Society, which
had its formal inauguration in Moscow on January 25,
1870. Thenceforth it was to be the headquarters of missionary work throughout the Russian Empire. Innokenty

likewise instituted mission celebrations with sermons and collections to be held annually in all parishes on the "Sunday of Orthodoxy." In this way he imbued the entire Church with the spirit that had dominated his own tremendous missionary activity: the conviction that all Orthodox Christians were obligated to participate in missions in one way or another.

By the end of his life—he died in 1879—Innokenty had built a firm ecclesiastical foundation for the principle of missionary work. However, the missionary activities of the Russian Orthodox Church were not destined to come to full flowering; the Bolshevik Revolution of 1917 put an end to all such projects. Since then the transformation of communications and the industrial development of Siberia have resulted in vast population shifts. Huge new industrial centers have sprung up, vast tracts of land have been put to the plow, and hordes of Russian engineers, workers and peasants have poured into Siberia. The whole nature of the missionary problem in Siberia has consequently changed. The present Orthodox Church of Russia, persecuted for so many years and lacking recruits, has proved unable to cope with this new situation.

The work of Innokenty represents only one small segment of the enormous, quiet, self-sacrificing work on the part of Russian Orthodox missionaries. The establishment of Orthodox churches in Peking, Japan and Korea, which survive to this day, is testimony to the effectiveness of this mission beyond the borders of Russia herself.

Linguistic Achievements of the Russian Orthodox Mission

The intellectual, cultural and civilizing role of Orthodoxy's tenacious, determined missionary work emerges most strikingly in the missionaries' linguistic achievements. It is owing to their translations that the languages of the most important peoples of Central and Far Eastern Russia acquired the status of literary languages. Not even the Soviet Encyclopedia can conceal this fact. Its article on the languages of the peoples of the USSR pays tribute to the philological work of the missionaries, whose inventiveness and vitality were exceptional. In the Volga region and throughout the whole of central and northern Siberia as far as Kamchatka, the Kuriles and Alaska, but also in the Caucasus and around the Aral Sea and Lake Baikal, alphabets were devised and translations forged in hitherto nonliterary languages. In the case of most of these nomadic peoples the missionaries found it necessary to incorporate some Byzantine or Old Church Slavonic words into the native languages, which naturally had no expressions for elements of Christian worship and doctrine. In this they were following the same policy as Wulfila had adopted in translating the Bible into Gothic. The Soviet Encyclopedia criticizes these missionaries for not having created a language that could cope with the world of modern technology, politics and science. But this charge is sheer anachronism; such topics did not come within the purview of missionaries or natives at the time the missions were conducted. The creative role of a translation of the Bible into a new language, on which we have commented earlier (see p. 107), must not be disregarded. The achievement of the Orthodox missionaries was stupendous, if only on that score.

9. THE NESTORIAN MISSION ON ASIATIC SOIL

Among the old schismatic churches of Asia, the best known is that of the Nestorians, adherents of the theological views of Nestorius, the Patriarch of Constantinople in 428–31. This doctrine lived on for centuries in the East Syrian theological school of Edessa, which exerted an extraordinary influence upon Christians in Persia, India and central Asia (see p. 80).

The Persian Church and Its Missionary Work

The Christians of Mesopotamia at first were under the authority of the Patriarch of Antioch. Since their country was part of Persia, it became necessary for them to have an independent head of their own church. This primate, or catholicos as he was called, resided from the beginning of the fifth century in what was then the capital of the Persian Empire, the huge twin city of Seleucia-Ctesiphon on the Tigris. A synod held in this city in 424 affirmed the independence of the new church from the Patriarch of Antioch. In matters of dogma, too, the Persian Church henceforth went its own way and officially espoused the doctrines of Nestorius. When in 489 the Eastern Roman emperor closed down the theological school of Edessa, the teachers fled to Persian territory. The vast expanses of the Persian Empire, which included the Land of the Two Rivers between Euphrates and Tigris, and all the land from Armenia to the Persian Gulf, offered the Nestorians an enormous field for missionary work. What was more, the political and commercial ties of Persia extended into central Asia and India. The Nestorians profited so well by the chance thus offered to them that from the seventh to the eleventh centuries the Nestorian Church had spread over more territory than any other Christian Church; it held sway over an area many times that of the Western Catholic Church. Its twenty-seven metropolitanates and thirty-two dioceses, containing many millions of believers, stretched from eastern Syria across Mesopotamia and Iran eastward as far as South India, southwest as far as Arabia. Yemen, too, belonged to the Persian Empire in those days, and in the capital of Sana and on the island of Sokotra, Nestorian bishops continued to be active down to the tenth century. Their influence upon the still-pagan Arabs was very considerable. Modern research has shown beyond a doubt that Muhammad, the founder of Islam, was deeply influenced by Nestorian teachings.

Throughout the whole period of the Sassanid dynasty the Persian Church was never a state Church in the same sense as the Church of the Byzantine Empire. Rather, it was consistently persecuted by the Sassanid rulers, who were themselves followers of the ancient Zoroastrian religion. A measure of reconciliation and toleration was attained under King Yazdegerd I (399–420). But its very history of persecution kept the Nestorian Church spiritually mobile and sharpened its sense of mission.

Later, when Muhammadanism came to eastern Syria and Mesopotamia, the Nestorian Church suffered severe numerical losses, but the ecclesiastical organization never crumbled. In fact, the Nestorians were the one Christian community toward whom the Muslims showed some favor. When the seat of Islam's caliph was transferred to Baghdad, the Nestorian catholicos also repaired there. He was considered the spokesman for all the Christians in the caliph's domains; that is to say, his position corresponded with that assigned to the Byzantine Patriarch in the Ottoman Empire after the fall of Constantinople.

The Nestorians of the caliphate became teachers, physicians and transmitters of the Greek classical heritage. They translated classical and Hellenistic philosophical, medical and scientific works. They paved the way for the Muslim Arabs to take over the heritage of Greek culture and science. This cultural work on the part of Nestorian Christianity was of the highest and most far-reaching importance, for after Greek philosophy and science had spread through the Islamic Orient it found its way back to Europe via the Moorish culture of Sicily and especially Spain. When the Latin Middle Ages rediscovered the works of Aristotle and of so many Greek scientists and physicians through Latin translations from the Arabic, they were receiving back the heritage that Oriental Christendom had transmitted to the Arabs during the sixth and seventh centuries. In those early centuries, too, Christianity had also spread over Transoxiana to Herat, Samarkand and China.

During the Islamic period Nestorian culture was centered in three cities: Nisibis, Gunde-Shapur and Merv. Nisibis was the site of a famous theological school founded by the Persian Narses—the creators of Syrian culture were for the most part of Persian origin. In Gunde-Shapur there arose a medical school that played a great part in the development of Arabic medicine. Merv, finally, was the principal cultural center for Transoxiana under the Sassanids. In the course of the Christianization of this country, numerous Christian works were translated into the language of the Sogdians, whose real homeland was the region around Samarkand and Bokhara, but who had early spread as far as Chinese Turkestan; there is evidence that the Sogdian literary language was in use in those parts in the second half of the first millennium. In translating the great body of Christian literature into this tongue, a modified form of the Syrian-Nestorian script was used.

Syrian culture continued to thrive during the period of Arab domination. In addition to theologians, the Nestorians produced great philosophers, physicians, jurists, historians and grammarians. The Nestorian doctors who were the caliph's personal physicians even wielded a certain amount of political influence, especially in the days of Harun-al-Rashid and his two successors. Frequently the caliphs entrusted high government offices to Christians.

Nestorian asceticism underwent curious changes, in consequence of the fact that marriage was highly prized in the Zoroastrian state religion of the Persian Empire and celibacy regarded as a religious crime. The Persian state passed numerous decrees penalizing monks and bishops for their celibacy. In the fifth century an anti-ascetic movement sprang up within the Nestorian Church. The *canones* of 485 gave monks the right to marry if they were not able to maintain a state of celibacy. At a council held in 499 it was decided that patriarchs and bishops might marry once, whereas the lower clergy were even permitted a second marriage. In the sixth century there was a reaction against the marriage of higher church dignitaries. The synod of 545 forbade the election of married persons as bishops or patriarchs. At the beginning of the same century a Mesopotamian monk named Abraham was sent from Kashkar to

Egypt to study Egyptian monasticism. Upon returning home he set up a strict monastic order modeled upon Egyptian practices, and henceforth became known as the "Father of monks." This reorganization of monasticism led to a fresh missionary drive.

The Nestorian anchorite movement seems to have spread to the heart of central Asia, for Cosmas Indicopleustes, the sixth-century Egyptian geographer, mentions monks and hesychasts[2] among the Bactrians, Huns, Indians, Perso-Armenians, Medes and Elamites. In the ninth century the Muslim dynasties of Persian origin, chief among which was the dynasty of the Samanids (874–999), penetrated central Asia. In accounts of Arabic writers of the Samanid period we find mention of the spread of Christianity in the region around Samarkand. In that area, however, Christianity had a formidable rival in Manichaeanism, which became established especially among the stable population of east Turkestan, who were more highly civilized than the nomadic Turkish tribes. But Christianity also gained ground among the Turkish tribesmen of central Asia. When the Muslim ilkhans began to rule in east and west Turkestan—from the end of the tenth century on—Christians were no longer oppressed. Samarkand remained the seat of a Nestorian metropolitan.

The Orthodox and Nestorian Missions
in the Chinese Empire

Christianity penetrated China by two routes: by the caravan trails from the commercial centers of the Persian Empire, in which there were Christian episcopal seats; and by the sea route to and beyond India, where strong Christian communities had likewise developed in the trading ports of the Malabar coast. Legend has it that Christianity was introduced into China by the Apostle Thomas and his disciples, two of whom are said to have reached China in

2 See note p. 101.

A.D. 67. In his *Adversus gentes,* written around 300, Arnobius speaks of the Christian mission reaching as far as the "Seres." There is also a tradition that Archaeus, Archbishop of Seleucia-Ctesiphon (411–15) and Silas, Patriarch of the Nestorians (505–20) established metropolitanates in China. However, there are no confirmations of such tales and no documents or evidences of Christian activity in China before the Tang dynasty (618–907).

On the other hand, there is ample evidence for the presence of a Christian Church in China from the time of the Tang dynasty forward. Political conditions under this dynasty were especially favorable to the introduction of foreign religions. After a long period of division China was united under strong rulers whose dominion extended over an area that included China proper, Manchuria, Mongolia, north Korea, Tibet, Singkiang and parts of central Asia, India, Tongking and Annam. It was a time of vigorous commercial activity. India, central Asia, Persia, Mesopotamia and the Near East were linked with China by sea and caravan routes. Muslims, Zoroastrians and Jews were to be found at the court of the Chinese emperor, and it is no wonder that the presence of Christians is also mentioned. The most significant evidence is the famous Pillar Inscription of Sian, which was discovered in 1623 by workmen digging the foundations for a new building. The pillar had been erected in 781 and the inscription contained the story of Nestorianism in China from its introduction, as well as a summary of the doctrines and practices of the missionaries. So astonishing was the content of this inscription that in Europe it was first taken to be a pious fraud on the part of Jesuit missionaries; they had, it was assumed, fabricated the inscription in order to date the presence of Christianity in China back to so early a time. Meanwhile, however, modern researches have unequivocally proved the genuineness of the pillar. It was erected by Ching Ching, who bore the Christian name Adam, and who is also mentioned in a Chinese Buddhist account as having collaborated with a Buddhist on the translation of a Buddhist sutra.

Ching Ching came from Balkh, present-day Afghanistan, and held a high position in the Chinese government. He had distinguished himself by suppressing a rebellion against the emperor.

Since the discovery of the pillar, other proofs of the existence of a Christian Church in China during the Tang dynasty have come to light. In the grottoes of Tun-huang in northwest China an inscription of a hymn to the Holy Trinity was discovered some years ago. This inscription also listed the names of a large number of Nestorian books and tracts which had either been written in Chinese or translated into that language. Finally, imperial edicts of the years 638, 745 and 843, found in Chinese records, mention the Nestorian Church, and Christian names are also to be found in Taoist sources.

The years 698 and 699 were marked by some violent Buddhist opposition to the "religion of light," and there were fresh difficulties in 713. Though tradition reports that in the period before 823 a metropolitan named David was consecrated for China, the fortunes of the Nestorian Church in China were no longer so bright.

In 843 the Emperor Wu Tsung, who was a devoted Taoist, issued a decree against Buddhism; Buddhist monks were ordered to return to civil life. This edict was simultaneously directed against the Nestorians. But the Church appears to have survived such harassments. An Arab who visited the capital of China in the ninth century was surprised to discover that the emperor knew of Noah, the prophets, Moses and Jesus, and possessed pictures of them. Nestorianism seems to have disappeared from Chinese soil around the end of the ninth century, however. On the other hand, it experienced a surprising revival in the Mongol Empire.

The Nestorian Mission in the Mongol Empire

Only very recently have we come to know something of the influence of Nestorianism upon the Mongol Empire. In general the Mongols have been considered destroyers of Christianity in Asia. But this notion is not quite accurate. It is true that the Mongols were directly responsible for the downfall of Asiatic Christianity, but the crushing of Christianity came only at the close of the dominion of the Mongols. During the first three centuries of Mongol rule the attitude of the Great Khans toward Christianity was exceedingly tolerant. The khan himself and the members of the imperial house leaned toward Christianity, Buddhism or Islam, depending on their personal attitudes. So strong was the influence of Christianity upon the Mongol imperial house that for long periods in the history of the Mongol Empire direct coalitions with Byzantium or Rome could be formed and joint action taken against the Muhammadan ilkhans. It was not until the reign of Tamerlane (Ta-Mir-Lan) that the Mongol Empire aligned itself with Islam.

Mongol Negotiations with Rome

We possess rather precise information about the position of the Nestorians in the Mongol Empire because Pope Innocent IV (1243–54) entered into diplomatic relations with the Mongol khans. Innocent IV wished to enforce worldwide recognition of the authority of the Church. His bold program had three principal points. These were: 1) continuation of the Crusade in Palestine; 2) extension of papal authority to the Eastern Church by diplomacy rather than by conquest; 3) rapprochement with the Mongols in order to convert them to Christianity. In pursuit of this program he sent a band of missionaries to Mongolia. Their leader was one Giovanni di Piano Carpini, and they arrived at the court of Guyuk in Karakorum on July 22, 1246. A report was soon dispatched to Rome. The prognosis for their mission was highly favorable, for the papal envoys found a large number of Nestorian Christians occupying influential posts. As for the Mongol khan, Carpini had the most encouraging news: "Christians who belong to his household assure us that they are firmly convinced the emperor is on the point of becoming a Christian."

By 1247 substantial progress had been made in the alliance, and Guyuk himself may have become a convert to the Nestorian Church. The chief of the Mongol army in the west, Alyigiday, was ordered to negotiate with the Christian powers. King Louis IX, the leader of the Christian crusaders, arrived in Cyprus and was there met by emissaries of Alyigiday to discuss joint military efforts for the "liberation" of the Christians in Palestine. Our knowledge of these negotiations is extraordinarily precise, for we know that Alyigiday's envoys reached Cyprus on December 14, 1248, and were received by King Louis on December 20. Louis IX soon afterward sent an embassy of his own, headed by André de Lonjumeau, to Alyigiday's camp.

The Mongols then prepared to conquer Syria, the venture being represented as a Crusade. Kublai Khan appointed a successful Mongol general named Kitboga for the task. Kitboga was a Nestorian Christian and could count on the sympathies of the Orthodox Christians of the Near East in a struggle against the Muslims. The military factors of the "Yellow Crusade," however, were weighted on the side of Islam, for when the Egyptian and Mongol armies met in Galilee on September 3, 1260, the battle ended with the complete defeat of the Mongols. Kitboga himself was captured and executed, and all hopes for Mongol expansion in the Near East were blasted. Islam was now the undisputed victor in that entire region, with the result that the Christian Church on Syrian soil was further suppressed, and the remnants of the Latin crusaders' states in Palestine were utterly routed.

Nevertheless, Christian influence remained a potent factor at the court of the Mongol emperor, and the khans had

friendly ties with the Christian powers of the West. Kublai
Khan became a convert to Buddhism but continued to
manifest great respect for Christianity. The Nestorian
Church enjoyed complete freedom in his empire. Roman
Catholics were also admitted to his lands. The Mongol
khans in Persia, too, were eager for rapprochement with
the Christians. In 1267 Abaga Khan sent his congratula-
tions to Pope Clement IV on his victory over Manfred,
the Hohenstaufen King of Sicily. The Nestorians in the
Middle East undertook to establish closer ties between the
Mongols and the Christian West. With Abaga Khan's ap-
proval, two Nestorian clerics attended the Council of Lyon
in 1274. The most important of the liaison men between
Kublai Khan and the Vatican were the three Venetian mer-
chants, Maffio and Niccolo Polo and the latter's son Marco
Polo. Maffio and Niccolo first reached China in 1262. In
1266 Kublai sent them back to Europe with a request to
the Pope to send a hundred Christian scholars and tech-
nicians to China to instruct his subjects in Western religion
and culture.

The benevolent attitude of the Council of Lyon toward
the plans for Mongol-Christian collaboration in the Near
East was interpreted by the ilkhans, the Mongol rulers of
Persia and Asia Minor, as confirmation of an alliance between themselves and the papal Curia. The West, however,
had no means to provide the ilkhans with military support.
In this period a more intensive diplomatic intercourse took
place between the Mongol khanate and the West than was
to be achieved ever afterward, though neither side gave
practical military aid to the other.

Christian Influences at the Court of the Mongol Khans

The medieval West had highly exaggerated views of the
Christian sympathies of the Mongol khans. The reason for
this was the fact that the bitterest enemies of the Mongol
Empire in West Asia were Muslims. In Western eyes the
central citadel of Islam was Mamluk Egypt, which the

Mongols had so frequently fought but never conquered. Because the Christians were enemies of Islam, the Mongol viceroys of Persia, the ilkhans, showed them favor. Three Persian viceroys had been baptized as Christians in their childhood; several of them had Christian wives who exerted a rather considerable influence upon them; and for a time the Mongols seemed to be balanced so precariously between Islam and Christianity that it appeared as though the lightest touch might sway the decision. The West regarded the Mongol khans as to some extent the successors of the mysterious Prester John, the legendary great Christian priest-king of the Far East. The pious legends and prophecies of the West revolved about the hope that Prester John would overrun the lands of Islam from the east while the crusaders attacked them from the west.

We possess an account of the religious tolerance of Great Khan Mangu from the pen of William of Rubruck, a Flemish Franciscan monk who in 1253 was sent by Louis IX of France to the court of the Great Khan in Karakorum. William relates that the Great Khan organized religious discussions among representatives of western Christianity, Buddhism and Nestorianism. And Mangu Khan himself attended Nestorian services, although he had not been baptized.

Thus there took place under the Mongols a moderate revival of that Nestorian Christianity that had flourished in China during the Tang dynasty and then had almost completely disappeared. In 1275 a Nestorian metropolitan was installed in Cambaluc, as Peking was known in medieval times. Nestorian Christians became so numerous and widely disseminated in the Mongol Empire that Kublai Khan in 1289 set up a special board, a kind of ministry of church affairs, especially for them. By 1330 the Archbishop of Soltania was reporting that there were more than 30,000 Nestorians in Cathay, and that they "were wealthy, with many handsome and richly decorated churches and crosses and images in honor of God and his saints. They held special divine services in the presence of the Emperor and had been granted great privileges by him." Chinkiang was one center of the Nestorians. There and in the vicinity Mar Sergius (Sargis), a physician from Samarkand who served as governor of the city in 1277–78, founded seven monasteries. At the beginning of the fourteenth century there were three Nestorian churches in Yangchow; one of them, the Church of the Cross, had been founded by a rich Nestorian merchant named Abraham at the end of the thirteenth century.

VIII.

Orthodox Culture

1. IS THERE AN ORTHODOX CULTURE?

Since the Orthodox religion profoundly affects the believer in his practical and intellectual attitudes toward God, his fellowmen and nature, it is obvious that an Orthodox culture must necessarily emerge from the Orthodox faith. Unfortunately there has so far been no comprehensive account of this Orthodox culture, in all the diversity of its forms, among the various Orthodox peoples of Greek, Slavic and Asiatic tongues. While the various types of thought and the social and cultural manifestations of the Western forms of Christianity have been the subject of scholarly examination—especially in the works of Ernst Troeltsch and Max Weber—similar studies of the Orthodox Church have been undertaken only with regard to Byzantine culture by Louis Bréhier, and those were confined to the Church of the Duchy of Kiev and the old Duchy of Moscow up to 1459. Yet the specific forms of Orthodox culture are much more obvious and much easier to identify than, say, the forms of Protestant culture, which very frequently appear in the guise of elusive, purely psychological variants. Orthodox culture finds expression far more openly and concretely not only in philosophy, literature and art, but also in habits of life and forms of community organization—down even to such matters as the peculiarly Orthodox cuisine. We can only suggest the bare outlines of Orthodox culture here. Certain exceptions must be noted. In both the Byzantine Empire and the old schismatic churches of Asia and Africa three areas of art do not fall within the sphere of Orthodox culture. These are: sculpture, the theater, and instrumental music for the Church. To compensate for these exceptions, however, other branches of art have been brought to an extraordinarily high development.

2. EXCEPTIONS
AND THE COMPENSATION FOR THEM

The Absence of Sculpture from Ecclesiastical Art

The absence of sculpture is due to a prohibition of its use in ecclesiastical art which—as we have shown in Chapter I—is connected with the theological conception of the nature of icons. The celestial archetypes are reflected only in the two-dimensional surfaces of icons (see p. 6). So strong have been the influence of the antisculptural spirit of Byzantine ecclesiastical painting and the effects of the iconoclastic controversy that Byzantine culture has never even developed secular sculpture. Sculpture has developed only in miniature art; but even there it has been confined largely to the art of relief, often an extremely shallow relief that in effect was scarcely removed from the two-dimensionality of the icons.

The ancient ecclesiastical art of ivory carving was practiced to a considerably greater extent. In the age of Justinian and the period immediately following single or double and triple foldable ivory tablets (diptychs and triptychs), and ivory boxes (pyxides) of classical beauty were produced; and in the Middle Ages also icons on single tablets of ivory, or diptychs and triptychs representing saints or Biblical motifs, were made in large numbers. There were also boxes, chests and bowls made for secular purposes but carved with ecclesiastical motifs. This type of art took root throughout the whole area under the influence of the Orthodox Church, not only in Asia Minor but also in the East and South Slavic lands. To supply the demand for liturgical vessels, a goldsmith's art of remarkable beauty grew up on Orthodox soil. To further embellish their creations, the goldsmiths early borrowed the Persian technique of enameling. The popular art of enameled metalwork, which was especially esteemed in Russia, was a direct outgrowth of this technique.

Icon Painting and Mosaics

The restriction of ecclesiastical art to two-dimensional painting had its positive as well as its negative aspect. It led to a great flowering of icon painting, to mural painting on the grandest scale, and above all to magnificent mosaic art. Christian mosaic art, of course, started from the base laid down by classical antiquity's approach to form and nature; but by abstract stylization according to intellectual and religious dictates, by abolishing realism and the illusion of space, an entirely new style was created. Ultimately all suggestion of space was either eliminated or only sketchily implied, and sculptural rounding of bodies shunned as far as possible; where a sense of space was suggested at all, the perspective was inverted, the focus of the lines not being in the eye of the observer, but at some transcendent point behind the picture—shifted, as it were, to the divine eye. The spatial lines ran from the observer back to this transcendental center; from this inverted, divine perspective, the human persons in the foreground of the picture were rendered smaller than the figures of the saints who, being closer to God, occupied the greater part of the icon's surface.

As it happens, works of Byzantine mosaic art and mural

paintings are now to be found almost exclusively in the West, largely in Ravenna and the Byzantine churches of Sicily. In the East they were mostly destroyed by the barbarous iconoclasts. A large number of mosaics, especially in the Balkans, were coated with whitewash by the Turkish conquerers of those regions. Some few escaped that fate, including the mosaics of the monastery church on Sinai (sixth century), the Churches of St. George (fifth century) and St. Demetrius (sixth to tenth centuries) in Salonika, the mosaics of Aya Sophia in Salonika (ninth century) and the earliest mosaics of the Koimesis church in Nicaea (presumably from the seventh century). Splendid examples of early medieval Byzantine mosaics are to be seen in Hosios Lukas in Stiris, in Nea Moni on Chios, in the monastic church of Daphni near Athens, and in the Kahriyeh Jamissi in Constantinople. In the West there are great mosaics in San Marco in Venice, in the Martorana in Palermo, and in the Cathedrals of Cefalù and Monreale. On Slavic soil, mosaic works of the eleventh century are preserved in the Churches of St. Sophia and St. Michael in Kiev.

Mural Painting

The iconoclasts of the eighth and ninth centuries wreaked even greater havoc upon mural painting. Nevertheless considerable series of murals have survived in the almost inaccessible cave churches of monks and eremites, who were in any case the firmest advocates of the veneration of images and often defended themselves against the iconoclasts by force of arms. Thus paintings on Latmos near Herakleia and especially in the numerous cave churches of Cappadocia, near Göreme and Ürgüb (ninth to eleventh centuries), escaped destruction. In the West the remains of frescoes in St. Saba in Rome (tenth century) and the great cycle of frescoes of St. Angelo in Formis near Capua (eleventh century) convey an impression of the grandeur of this mural painting. There are also mural paintings in

Novgorod (twelfth century), in Mirosh near Pskov
(twelfth century) and in the Church of the Redeemer at
Neredichy (c. 1200).

The art of the fourteenth and fifteenth centuries is especially well represented. There are, for instance, the ex-
tensive series of paintings in the churches of Mistra and in
a number of monasteries on Athos, as well as in many
Serbian, Macedonian and Romanian monasteries. Strong
Cretan influences are evident in these latter. Cretan icon
and mural painting exerted an indirect influence upon the
baroque art of the West in the seventeenth century, for the
Greek painter Domenicos Theotocopoulos, known to the
West as El Greco, carried thither the traditions of the icon
and mural painting of his native Crete.

Careful restoration projects by art experts in the past few
decades have uncovered a goodly number of the Byzantine mosaics and murals which the Turks had attempted to
bury beneath coats of whitewash and plaster. The results
of such restoration in Salonika make us once more aware
of the overwhelming variety and splendor of Byzantine art.
In fact Salonika with its multitude of churches of many
periods is the best place to visit if we would form some conception of the whole span of Byzantine art from the fifth to
the fourteenth centuries. There are also the many churches
in Berrhoea in Greek Macedonia whose art has likewise
been revealed once more. The most staggering sight of all,
however, is afforded by the resurrected mosaics of the
greatest miracle of Byzantine ecclesiastical architecture,
Hagia Sophia, the heart of the Byzantine Church. The great
church was transformed into a mosque after the conquest
of Constantinople in 1453. At last, under the enlightened
rule of Kemal Pasha, the edifice was made a Turkish national museum and the mosaics of the dome, dating from
the golden age of Byzantine supremacy that followed on the
end of the iconoclastic struggle, now glow once more in
their original beauty.

Metallic Adornment of Icons

The art of icon painting was to some degree the loser when the custom arose—especially in Slavic countries—of expressing veneration for the sacred image by embellishing it with costly metals and gems. Thus the icons are frequently coated with gold leaf or hammered silver, with the outlines of the holy figures incised or pricked into the rich ground, only their hands and faces being painted. Other metals, such as bronze, copper and tin, might be used, or else the icon might be made of a plaque of wood into which the sacred figures were carved. Enameling was also greatly favored. Through the dissemination of icons in every house, from mansion to hovel, these art forms of the Orthodox Church have had the most enormous influence upon the aesthetic feelings of the Orthodox populace.

Illumination

Alongside of icon and mural painting there was also the flourishing art of illumination. Theologians and monks read the Fathers of the Church in richly ornamented manuscripts; priests and choir studied beautifully illuminated copies of the liturgy. Fostered by generous commissions from the emperors and numerous donors, illumination developed into an art of the greatest magnificence throughout the whole territory of the Orthodox Church. The treasuries of the monasteries on Athos and Mount Sinai, which have only recently been opened to inspection, are filled with gloriously embellished manuscripts of psalters, liturgical documents and writings of the Fathers.

Minor Arts and Crafts

The minor arts and crafts were also brought to a high peak of perfection in Byzantium. Much of both Arabian craftsmanship and that of the West stem from this source. The West is particularly indebted to Byzantium for two important crafts. The first of these is the art of pouring bronze, a classical technique that was kept alive in the Byzantine Empire. Bronze doors, baptismal fonts and bowls of great artistic value were produced; and in the eleventh and twelfth centuries the technique was transplanted to Sicily and southern Italy (Amalfi). Byzantine bronzes manifested the characteristic Eastern tendency to stress two-dimensionality in sacred images.

An equally important craft was that of silk weaving, which took over the images and stylistic motifs of icon painting and developed these into an independent art. The weavers wrought veritable miracles in the production of altar cloths and liturgical robes. Similarly in Ethiopia, Georgia, Armenia and Egypt the rug makers borrowed images and stylistic motifs from icon painting.

Carolingian art found its inspiration in the whole compass of Byzantine art, from icon and mural painting to illumination and the designing of liturgical robes (consider the dalmatic of Charlemagne in St. Peter's in Rome). The Arabian crafts that spread out over the Iberian Peninsula were also strongly affected both in their techniques and in their styles by Byzantine examples. Arabian illumination plainly reveals such influences. In fact, as Frobenius has shown, Byzantine art left its stamp as far south as the Nubian cultures of central Africa.

3. LACK OF THEATER. FLOURISHING OF LITURGY

The early Christians regarded the theater as a spawning ground of pagan ideas. Tragedy as a rule dealt with the myths of the old gods; comedy represented licentiousness in all its forms. Almost all the great Fathers of the Church condemned the theater in their sermons and writings and endeavored to keep Christians from attending it. A distaste for theater as a resort of demons, idolatry and lewdness became deeply rooted in the Church. The older Church ordinances—particularly in Egypt—listed the profession of actor together with that of brothel keeper, judge and soldier among the occupations that a man must abandon if he wished to receive baptism. Consequently there was never any chance for theater to develop in the area of Byzantine culture. Not until the eleventh century was any Christian drama attempted: *The Suffering Christ,* an enactment of the Passion. But this effort was not intended for the stage; it was a crude literary construct, a so-called *cento,* that is, a play composed of verses and fragments of verses pieced together out of classical tragedy. Such erudite pastiches can scarcely be regarded as the rebirth of tragedy in the Byzantine Empire.

In compensation for the extinction of classical drama, an extraordinary wealth of liturgy developed in the Church. This liturgy—as we have indicated on p. 34—is a highly animated mystery play, with various entrances and processions and responsive choruses. Each particular church could give its own turn to these mystery dramas, since for a long time there were no curbs on improvisation. It was not until the nineteenth century that a native secular drama finally appeared, and then it was only in the western Orthodox countries, primarily in Russia, which were receptive to current Western literary influences. Otherwise, ecclesiastical tradition almost completely suppressed the birth of secular drama.

On the other hand, the essentially dramatic nature of the liturgy led to the continual creation of a host of new forms; the original character of the liturgy as charismatic improvisation went on exerting a creative influence even after the form of the liturgy itself had been more or less frozen by the imposing of uniform patterns upon the whole of the Byzantine state Church. In the various churches of Byzantium the sermon became a kind of dramatized homily. That is to say, the commentary on particular Gospel texts was enlivened by insertion of dialogues, little scenes, monologues and choruses. Various episodes out of the Bible were incorporated into the general mystery drama of the liturgy.

There would be, for example, an enactment of the baptism of Jesus, of the childhood of Mary, of the Annunciation, of the conspiracy of the demons against Christ, of the birth of Christ, of the flight to Egypt, or of Christ's harrowing of hell. These dramatic representations were closely linked with the liturgy of particular church festivals; they were inserted amid the rituals of the feast day; and the actors were not laymen, but clerics, usually the same priests and deacons who celebrated the liturgy. Comic and grotesque motifs crept into such performances; in fact, the restrictions that were finally set upon the dramatization of the liturgy were in answer to these exuberances of the imagination. Similar development of the mystery play took place in the West, of course; but in Byzantium, religious drama was never allowed to drift away from its liturgical, ecclesiastical origins.

4. THE BAN ON INSTRUMENTAL MUSIC FOR THE CHURCH. ASCENDANCY OF CHORAL SINGING

The Dogmatic Justification

The Orthodox Church excluded instrumental music from its observances on dogmatic grounds: Man must not employ lifeless metals and lifeless wood to praise God. Rather, he himself should be the living instrument for the praise of God. He should not delegate his Christian task to flutes, trumpets and organs, but should glorify God with his own lips as also with his whole life. One important reason for this rejection of instrumental music was the fact that certain pagan mystery cults employed music to intensify the orgiastic mood of their rites. Consequently the Church held aloof from this music as representing a pagan form of worship, just as it did from the pagan theater. Thus, instrumental music in the Byzantine Empire was restricted to secular celebrations. Small portable organs were played at court festivals and in the circus, but not in church.

The Ascendancy of Choral Singing

The very absence of instrumental music led to an unusual proliferation of choral song and hymnody in the churches. Orthodox services are marked by an altogether extraordinary amount of music, and music of such technical difficulty that it can be handled only by trained choirs. Even the smallest Orthodox parish maintains a choir. These choirs are highly accomplished, if only because of the complicated demands of the liturgy and the immense repertoire of hymns of all types. It would lead us too far afield to analyze the different types of liturgical song which are designated by such names as *hirmoi, stichera, kontakia,* etc. Considerable demands also are made upon the vocal and musical talents of priests and deacons.

Up to the second half of the ninth century the authors of the hymns were poet-composers who created both words and music. There followed an era of hymn writers who set new poems to existing melodies. The eleventh century saw a new flowering of Byzantine music, characterized by extended coloratura passages; and this period passed directly into the neo-Greek era of hymn composition. In the Russian Church, in Greece, and especially on Greek islands with considerable Italian populations, monodic Byzantine music was replaced partly or completely by modern western European music with its harmony and polyphonic choral singing. In present-day Greece both Byzantine music and italianized polyphonic music are equally favored. The monasteries, especially those on Mount Athos, preserve the old monodic style, but modern polyphonic choral singing is well entrenched in the great cathedrals of Athens, Salonika and Corinth. In Russia the time-honored monodic style has been retained by the Old Believers, but the regular Orthodox Church has come under the sway of Italian music and polyphonic singing has almost entirely won out there. Some monodic hymns in the older Byzantine style, which grew out of the liturgical practice in Kiev, Novgorod or

Moscow, are still preserved. The great Russian composers of the past few centuries contributed enormously to the further development of ecclesiastical choral music, and church music in its turn has to some extent affected the secular works of Russian composers (for example, Tschaikovsky).

Since many of the villagers or townspeople of Orthodox parishes participated in the church choir, such choral singing also exerted considerable influence upon folk songs in the Orthodox countries. Stylistic elements of Byzantine hymns can be detected in many Greek folk songs; and similarly, Russian folk songs in many respects reflect the style of Russian Orthodox church music. In the Syrian Orthodox Church as well as in the Monophysite and Nestorian churches in Asia and Africa, the liturgical song of the fifth century has been preserved right down to the present; and in these areas too the same relationship between church music and folk songs may be observed.

IX.

The Ethical Ideas of Orthodoxy

1. INADEQUACY OF RESEARCH

We have already had occasion to observe that the whole subject of Orthodox culture has scarcely been given adequate treatment by historians and sociologists. This is even more true of the ethical ideas of Orthodoxy. Up to the present, the whole problem of ethics, especially of the social ethics of Orthodoxy, has hardly been subjected to systematic historical investigation. We should by no means conclude from the insufficiency of such studies that a social ethic does not exist. Quite the contrary. The ideas and impulses of Christian social ethics operate with particular force within Orthodox theology, as any systematic account can make plain.

Since the whole field of Orthodox ethics has been extraordinarily confused by modern political slogans, we must begin by distinguishing three elements: first, the socioethical principles expressed in the Orthodox interpretation of Christianity, that is to say, chiefly in Orthodox dogmatics and liturgy; second, the social doctrines that have been developed by Orthodox ecclesiastics or theologians as direct contributions to social problems; and third, the effects of Orthodox socioethical ideas upon various philosophical, political, social and cultural reform movements, especially in the history of Russian thought.

2. THE ETHICS OF LOVE

Orthodoxy has given certain elements of Christian social ethics a special interpretation that has left its impress upon history. In line with Johannine Christianity, Orthodoxy stresses brotherly love, not only for all believers but also for all men. The idea springs from the conception that all men are created after the image of God, that Christ died for all, and that all are called to the resurrection in the new life.

Brotherhood, too, stems from the real center of the religion of the Eastern Church; the Eucharistic liturgy, the participation of all the baptized in the wedding supper that makes them members of the Mystical Body of Christ. Uniting in the Eucharist with the resurrected Lord and with the celestial Church of angels and saints, the earthly Church becomes a community of brothers. Consequently, before communion the Eucharistic liturgy proclaims the mutual forgiveness of all sins "in words, in works or thoughts, on this day or on all the days of my life."

The Russian writer Gogol in his famous *Observations on the Divine Liturgy* (1847) pointed up the moral implications of this brotherhood forming in the presence of Christ. After the mutual forgiveness of sins the priest cries out: "Christ is in the midst of us," and the deacon replies: "He is and will be." Gogol observes: "Formerly, all those assembled in the church used to kiss one another, men the men and women the women, saying: 'Christ is in the midst of us!' and answering: 'He is and will be!' That tradition persists, though in a modified form, for every communicant summons to his mind all Christians, not only those in the temple at the time, but the absent ones also, not only those close to his heart, but also those who have remained remote from it; hastening to reconcile himself with all those toward whom he has felt envy, hatred or discontent, he gives them all a kiss in spirit, saying to himself: 'Christ is in the midst of us,' and answering on their behalf: 'He is and will be!' Unless he does this he will be dead to all the holy acts that follow, after the words of Christ himself: 'Leave your gift there before the altar and go; first be reconciled to your brother, and then come and offer your gift'; and after the words of Christ's apostle: 'If any one says, "I love God," and hates his brother, he is a liar; for he who does not love his brother whom he has seen, cannot love God whom he has not seen.' "

It is probably the Easter liturgy that most vividly expresses this idea of fraternity. The kiss of peace of the primitive Church has been retained in this Easter liturgy to symbolize the mutual forgiveness of sins and the forging of a community freed of all guilts and desires for vengeance. (That kiss has vanished from the ordinary Sunday liturgy of the Byzantine Church, but it continues in the Coptic, Ethiopian, Armenian, Nestorian and Syrian-Jacobite churches.) On Easter Sunday the choir sings: "The Day of Resurrection. Let the festival of the people illuminate us. And let us embrace one another. Let those who hate us speak to us: 'Brethren, for the sake of the Resurrection we will all forgive one another'; and so let us cry out: 'Christ rose from the dead after destroying death by death; he gives life to all those resting in their tombs.' " This sense of the mystical union of all the redeemed in their participation in the resurrected Lord is the innermost core of Orthodox collective and individual ethics, and is continually kept alive by the mystery of the Eucharist.

3. HAS ORTHODOX ETHICS FAILED IN FINDING SOLUTIONS TO THE SOCIAL PROBLEM?

It might be imagined that this emphasis upon the Christian ethics of brotherly love would have decisively affected social conditions in the Orthodox countries. That had been the case in the era of the primitive Church, when the spiritual teachers and leaders of the various churches were forever admonishing their flock concerning the social responsibilities of Christians. After Christianity became the state religion of the Roman Empire, the Church assumed the task of reminding the Christian emperors of their social obligations. The Church itself established hospitals and charitable institutions of all kinds, and constantly urged upon the wealthy their duty to the poor.

Unfortunately, there were other forces that worked against this current as Church and state became more and more interlocked. As time went on, the state Church put itself more at the service of political absolutism, which was anchored in the principle of divine right. Gradually the Church withdrew from all but purely charitable social activity. It became a principle of Orthodoxy to remain aloof from politics, so that even in the eventful nineteenth century the Russian Orthodox Church—and this was one of its greatest tragedies—made scarcely any significant contribution toward a solution of the glaring social inequities in tsarist Russia.

We must add a reservation to the above statement: on this point there exists an almost total gap in historical research. No historian has looked into the part played by the Church in the liberation of the serfs in the mid-nineteenth century or has attempted to discover what position it took on the social question toward the end of that century. Nor are there any studies of the role assumed by the Russian Orthodox Church in the Revolutions of 1905 and 1917. What histories we have, give the impression that all Russian social problems of the nineteenth and early twentieth centuries were completely ignored by the Church. Certainly the most famous advocate of social reform founded upon Christianity, Leo Tolstoy, stood in bitter opposition to the Orthodox Church, and drew many of his reformist ideas from German, English and American Protestantism. On the other hand, we must consider the large and influential group of Slavophiles, whose ideals and ideas for reform were based on Orthodox principles, above all upon the idea of *sobornost*.[1]

4. IDEAS OF SOCIAL REFORM IN ORTHODOX RUSSIA

It would be most unfair to regard the Russian Church as having failed totally to meet its social responsibilities. Within the Orthodox Church during the nineteenth and twentieth centuries there were always individuals, priests and devout laymen, who were stirred by the urgent social questions to seek solutions in the spirit of Christian ethics. The Church as an institution, however, was shackled, as were the theological seminaries. The official Church was bent upon asserting the legitimacy of reactionary cultural and social policies within the Russian Empire. Social protest came not from the higher clergy or the accredited theologians, but from individuals among the lower clergy and laymen; it came chiefly, however, from the Old Believers (*Raskolniki*) and other sectarians who for centuries had been denouncing the state and the state Church, which they identified with Antichrist. These sectarians considered the changes in the Russian Church that had taken place under Patriarch Nikon (1605–81) a betrayal of the true spirit of Orthodoxy.

The Lower Clergy

Little has been written about the Christian social ideas that emerged from the lower clergy. All that is known is that the seminaries where Russian priests received their training became spawning grounds of revolutionary and

[1] *Sobornost* is the key theological concept of Russian Orthodoxy. The word was originally the Old Church Slavonic translation of the Greek *ecclesia* (church) and signified community in Christ.

social-reformist ideas. These seminaries usually offered the sole chance for education and improvement of social status to the often highly gifted young men who were the sons of Russian priests. Not only the ideas of Christian social reform, but also modern radical, nihilist, atheistic and revolutionary programs found their way into the seminaries. Such leaders of Russian nihilism as Chernyshevsky and Dobrolyubov stemmed from priestly families and the seminaries. So did a number of the leaders of the Communist Revolution. Stalin first embarked on revolutionary activity in the days when he was a student at the Orthodox Seminary of Tiflis.

Grigory Petrov

Some Orthodox social reformers came into prominence at the turn of the century. One such figure was Grigory Petrov. Although a member of the established Orthodox Church, he was one of the most incisive social critics of his time. He published a newspaper called "God's *Pravda*"[2] which won so great a following among the Orthodox that it became a special target of the Marxists—chiefly of Lunacharsky, who was later to be People's Commissar of Education under the Bolshevik regime—who were fiercely opposed to anything resembling Christian socialism. Petrov was for a time spiritual tutor in the households of two grand dukes and was in line to being appointed tutor of Alexey, the heir to the throne, but changed course and became an opponent of the existing system. He was subsequently elected to the Duma, the first Russian parliament, as an independent. Petrov contended that the dominant political and social system of Russia could no longer pretend to be based upon the religious and ethical principles of the Russian Church. In an epistle addressed to Metropolitan Antony in 1908 he declared: "Neither Christian emperor, Christian government nor Christian social order exist. The

2 *Pravda* means "justice" as well as "truth" in Russian.

upper classes oppress the lower; a small group oppresses all the rest of the population. . . . This group has excluded the lower classes from everything: from power, science, art, even from religion. It has made religion its servant."

Petrov was most vehement in his attacks upon the attitude of the clergy, who were shirking their Christian responsibility for the social problems of their times. "Politics is first and foremost an affair of the Church. Indeed, it is the fundamental concern of the Church. True politics is the art of how best to build political and social life. And the Gospels with their doctrines of the Kingdom of God are the science of the best arrangement of political and social life." Petrov cried out against the role played by the Russian Church as a state institution: "But the Church did not transfigure the state. Instead, it borrowed superficial glitter from the state. . . . Christianity became the state religion, but the state did not, in consequence, cease to be pagan. . . . The explanation of this paradox is that the influence of Christianity was not directed to the political and social order. The Gospels were deflected from their broad mission of establishing the Kingdom of God in society and state into the narrow path of personal virtue and personal salvation." This was a major error. "The Church is a universal, supranational and suprapolitical organization. For the Church, none of the existing political systems is perfect, final and inviolable. Any such utopian political system remains a thing of the future: the coming Kingdom of God. This will be a regime not founded upon external compulsion, but upon inner bonds that are both universal and moral. It will be an order in which there will be no exploitation, no tyranny, no force, no masters and servants, and in which all will bear the burdens of life equally. . . . The achievement of such an order is the mission of the Church."

Writings of this sort show clearly that consciousness of social responsibility had not been entirely stamped out within the Russian Church. Here were the same ideas emerging in Russia that were simultaneously appearing in America in the form of the Social Gospel, and in Germany as a movement to recall the Church to its social obligations. It remains significant, however, that the Russian Orthodox Church did not heed these suggestions. Instead, the Church expelled Petrov from its midst because of his social-reformist ideas.

The Priest Gapon

In this connection we might also speak of another Orthodox priest whose name is remembered for his association with the Bloody Sunday of 1905. Gapon organized a procession of the populace who, bearing icons and pictures of the tsar, came to seek an audience with their tsar "to petition him for *pravda* in the Russian land." In past centuries the Orthodox tsar had represented divine *pravda;* large segments of the Christian populace were convinced that that golden era had ceased with the introduction of non-Orthodox principles of government by Peter the Great. They reasoned that the original intimate tie between the Orthodox tsar and his Orthodox people had been broken by the intervention of a non-Orthodox foreign class of intellectuals and officials. Gapon believed that this interference could be eliminated and *pravda* on earth restored so that the Orthodox tsar would once more be truly one with his Orthodox people. But on Bloody Sunday 1905 the Preobrashensky Regiment opened fire on the procession, killing hundreds upon hundreds of helpless people. Afterward, Gapon wrote: "I went to the Tsar in the simple-hearted belief that we would receive *pravda*. . . . I went at the head [of the procession], facing the bullets, to purchase with my blood the renewal of Russia and the establishment of *pravda*." In his eloquent proclamation of January 9, 1905, Gapon asserted that the shocking outcome of that well-meant demonstration signified the severing of the bond that had hitherto linked the Orthodox tsar with the Orthodox people. "The bullets of the Tsar's soldiers which killed the bearers of the Tsar's portraits riddled the portraits with holes and killed our faith in the Tsar." In a letter to the tsar, Gapon predicted the bloody horrors of the coming revolution.

Ideas of Social Reform in Russia
in the Revolution of 1917

While Gapon dreamed of restoring the Christian order by means of a change of heart in the ruling class, such reformers as Petrov had already expressed the thought that Orthodoxy was not necessarily tied to any specific governmental system—that is to say, to tsarism; that it must concern itself solely with the idea of achieving the kingdom of God in political and social life. Later, at the time of the Revolution of 1917, these arguments made it possible for numerous leaders of Orthodoxy to accept the overthrow of tsarism. At the All-Russian Synod of 1917, at which the constitution of the Russian patriarchate was restored, a number of the clergy and laymen present took up Petrov's ideas and applied them to the situation brought about by the revolution. Such ideas also influenced leading Christians among the Russian Mensheviks. Kerensky himself has repeatedly called attention to the Christian roots of his revolutionary ideas. Thus he writes in his autobiography: "I was profoundly impressed by the image of the resurrected Christ. . . . Everything led to the intimate association of religion with daily life. . . . In those early impressions, in those Biblical stories, in that image of the wonderful man who had given his life for others—there and nowhere else . . . was to be found the source of my passion for revolution."

5. ORTHODOX ROOTS
OF RUSSIAN BOLSHEVISM?

Socialism and Anticipation of the Kingdom of God

Many recent publications have advanced the thesis that the deepest roots of Russian Bolshevism are to be found in the Russian Orthodox religion. The authors of such works point especially to the Messianic ideas that circulated so freely in Russia, especially among the Old Believers and the various sects. These ideas, they maintain, prepared the masses of the people psychologically for a total overthrow of the existing order and for a radical, Communist reshaping of political and social conditions. The proponents of this thesis are wont to assert that the Orthodox conception of the Church, as expressed in the idea of sobornost, laid such stress upon collective salvation that no room was left for any genuine belief in the Christian person. In other words, it is argued, the individual had already been sacrificed to the collective within the framework of Christian ideas of community.

This notion represents a distortion of historical relationships. It must be granted that, taking modern intellectual history as a whole, an inner connection does exist between the Christian ideas of community at any given time and the political and social ideals of community. But this relationship can never be called one of cause and effect, nor can it be restricted to a specific nation. In the long history of the Christian Church, both East and West have repeatedly experimented with Christian communities, have sought to achieve the primitive Christian ideal of sharing of property as it is set forth in the Acts of the Apostles. Such attempts by Anabaptist, spiritualistic and other radical Christian sects both in Europe and America were early steps along the path of Christian socialism. They were all variations of the same endeavor to establish, or at least to prepare, the kingdom of God on earth.

One of the special features of the Christian idea of the kingdom of God is the linking of genuine personalism with the concept of a community of brotherly love—love being an act of freedom and creative spontaneity upon the part of redeemed man. The Orthodox conception of sobornost explicitly upholds this respect for personality and freedom as essential elements in the Christian community of love. Russian thinkers who made the ideal of sobornost the heart of their message, such as Khomiakov, were the most fervent advocates of Christian personalism; they charged the atheistic West with annihilating human personality. If, therefore, certain echoes of messianic and eschatological elements are to be heard in Russian Bolshevism, we cannot say that they represent traces of Russian Orthodoxy—not even if we call them "distortions" of the Orthodox heritage.

Sobornost and the Bolshevist Idea of Community

It is therefore quite wrongheaded to conclude that the idea of sobornost paved the way for a victory of collectivity over individuality. By the same reasoning one might declare that the Western concept of the Church as the Mystical Body of Christ promoted the spread of Marxism. The fact is that Orthodoxy in no way destroys, represses or devaluates individuality, but rather establishes an organic relationship between the individual and the community. There are, however, certain shades of difference between the Western and the Orthodox conceptions of this relationship. In the West, stronger emphasis is given to the importance of the individual personality, probably under the influence of Roman law, which so firmly defends the rights of the individual. By contrast, in Russia the principle of community has been stressed as against the special rights of the individual. But within Orthodoxy as well, individuality receives its due in the doctrine of personal resurrection and restitution. Orthodoxy adheres to the Christian view that the individual will not be dissolved in the Absolute at the final restitution. The Orthodox doctrine of sobornost achieves a nice balance. It avoids the West's occasional overemphasis on the claims of individuality which may end by alienating the person from the Mystical Body of Christ. On the other hand, it also avoids overvaluation of a collective that kills all individuality, such as has emerged from Bolshevist social doctrine. In the present situation—and this is all-important—Christianity in Russia is the sole support of personalism against the annihilation of individuality by the Bolshevist doctrine of man. There can be no doubt that the Bolsheviks, in their battle against the Orthodox Church from 1918 on, regarded the advocates of the Christian idea of sobornost as their worst enemies; and in turn the latter vehemently attacked, and are today continuing to attack, communism's ideal of community and the Communist view of man.

The only demonstrable connection between Russian Orthodoxy and Bolshevism is a negative one. That is to say, the intellectual degeneracy of the state Church served the ends of Bolshevist propaganda, for it could be represented as evidence of Marxism's thesis that religion is "the opium of the people." The character of the Russian Church in the nineteenth century truly made religion appear to be a narcotic handed out to the exploited populace by a priesthood serving the ruling class. The priests seemed to be dedicated to the task of stupefying the people and blocking cultural and educational progress on orders from their employers. But to represent Russian Bolshevism itself as a "native fruit" of Russian Orthodoxy is highly suspect. On the contrary, the fact is that Russian Bolshevism is a legitimate offspring of Marxism, and as such is directly descended from Western positivism, materialism and a gruesomely misunderstood Hegelianism. As for Bolshevism's political victory in Russia, this could not have been brought about without the assistance of the Western powers. We must recall that the German High Command transported Lenin from Switzerland to Russia, hoping that the kindling of Bolshevist revolution would prepare the ground for a separate peace with Germany. But it must also be remembered that the Allies, by calling off their armed intervention against Bolshevism and making separate agreements with the Bolshevist revolutionary government, furthered the internal victory of Bolshevism and helped to stabilize the regime.

Sobornost and Mir[3]

The Slavophiles assert that certain Communist social forms in Russia, especially collective farming, are related to the Orthodox ideal of sobornost. According to Samarin, these forms constituted "as it were the secular, historical side of the Church." This thesis is based upon a romantic and wholly unhistorical overestimation of the mir. In reality the agrarian communism of the mir had nothing whatsoever to do with Russian Orthodoxy. The system by which the land of a village community was repeatedly redivided among its members, and in which the community rather than the individual was responsible for the cultivation and yield of the common lands, was introduced in relatively modern times in Russia, as a practical device for simplifying taxation. It proved easier and more convenient to collect taxes from the village as a unit rather than from individual peasants. Similarly, it was easier to make the village responsible for forced labor for public purposes. The system was particularly promoted by the government after the abolition of serfdom, for once the peasantry had been freed, the landowner could no longer be charged with the responsibility of raising taxes. On this point the modern Russian Communist sociologists have obviously a better explanation for the origin of the mir than have the Slavophile romantics who want to see the mir as a secular reflection of the Orthodox sobornost.

6. THE SOCIAL ACTIVITY
OF THE ORTHODOX CHURCH OF GREECE

The failure of the Russian state Church during the nineteenth and twentieth centuries need not lead us to condemn

[3] Mir (Russ.) = communal village organization in which the land was periodically redivided among the members of the community and all members were jointly responsible for payment of the taxes.

the Orthodox Church in general for want of a social ethic. No such charge, for example, can be laid at the door of the Orthodox Church of Greece. On the contrary. The Greek Church has had to cope with two major historical disasters that befell the Greek people in our century as the result of the two world wars—the expulsion of Orthodox Greeks from Asia Minor after the First World War, and the occupation of Greece by Germans, Italians and Bulgarians during the Second World War, followed by Communist revolution and bloody struggles in northern Greece. Confronted with these catastrophes, the Greek Church threw itself with admirable spirit into social work and made significant contributions to the solution of the problems that beset the impoverished nation. The "Apostolic Deaconry" established by the Greek Orthodox Church proved to be an excellent instrument of social welfare which did not restrict itself to charitable measures alone, but worked within the framework of Christian social ethics for a general solution of social problems, and attempted to introduce Christian values into the social policies of the government. The social activities of the Greek Church are probably the strongest historical evidence to counter the vague charges of Orthodoxy's failures in the realm of social ethics. They also give the lie to any theories of the link between Bolshevism and the Orthodox ideas of community —for it becomes quite evident that the Orthodox doctrine of brotherly love may be realized within the framework of traditional government.

X.

The Political Ideas of Orthodoxy

The structural difference between the Roman Catholic Church and the Eastern Orthodox Church emerges nowhere so sharply as in the basic relationship of Church and state. We may best understand this difference by considering the two great theologians who forged these views in their respective realms of Christianity: Eusebius of Caesarea and St. Augustine.

1. EUSEBIUS OF CAESAREA: FATHER OF THE ORTHODOX IDEA OF ECCLESIASTICAL STATISM

Constantine as the Prototype of the Christian Emperor

Eusebius of Caesarea (†c. 339) was the court theologian of Constantine the Great. In his speeches and writings on Constantine, as well as in his *Ecclesiastical History,* Eusebius set his stamp upon the political attitudes of Orthodoxy and formed the Church's picture of its relationship with the state for many centuries to come. Eusebius' key conception was that of the *Imperium Christianum.* In this Eusebius was probably taking up the ideas of Constantine

himself. When Constantine founded the city of Constantinople, which he solemnly consecrated on May 11, 330,
under the name of New Rome, he was proclaiming his own
view of his position within the Empire and the Church. He
raised the city of Byzantium to the same rank as Rome,
and transferred to it the political and administrative institutions of Rome, including the Senate. In so doing, he
unequivocally indicated his intention to give the newly
Christianized Empire a new capital uncontaminated by
pagan traditions—a capital, moreover, which would cede
nothing to the old Rome in splendor, but which would not
be burdened by the "diabolic" powers of Rome's past.

Eusebius made this idea the basis of his political theology.
At the heart of this theocracy stood a Christian emperor
modeled upon Constantine. To Eusebius the Christian emperor was the vicar of God on earth; God himself had
made him "the image of his omnipotent autocracy." The
emperor was "beloved of God," "thrice blessed" servant
of the supreme Ruler, "armed with divine armor" and entrusted with the task of "cleansing the world of the band
of the godless." He was "the strong-voiced herald of the
inexorable fear of God," by whose radiance "he illuminates
the world." Not only was he the prototype of justice, but
also the prototype of humanitarian love. "Thus God himself, the supreme Ruler of the whole world, appointed Constantine the lord and leader of all, so that no man can boast
of having raised him up," Eusebius wrote, thus reposing
the rule of the Orthodox emperor directly upon divine
right. The directness of Constantine's relationship with God
was shown, according to Eusebius, by the fact that God
had not sent other men to instruct him but had personally
guided the emperor by inspiration and "miraculous heavenly visions."

Christian Transformation of Divine Emperorship

There is no doubt that Eusebius, in formulating the role
of the Christian emperor in this way, bestowed a virtual

Christian baptism upon the old Roman idea of divine emperorship. Many of Eusebius' statements are apt to be echoes of the cult of *Sol invictus,* the invincible sun god of the pagans, of whom the emperor was an earthly representative. Thus Eusebius wrote of Constantine: "As the sun rising from the globe of earth impartially lavishes all his rays of light, so Constantine, who emerged from the imperial palace at dawn, as though to appear simultaneously with the beacon of the sky, cast over all who came before his countenance the radiance of his goodness." This emperor, like the pagan god-emperor who held the office of *Pontifex Maximus* in the Roman state religion, occupied the central position within the Church as well as the government. It was he who called the councils of bishops "as if God had appointed him bishop of all others," who presided over the synods and made their decrees legally binding upon Empire and Church. He was the protector of the Church who would defend the unity and truth of the Christian faith, not only as a warrior, but also as an intercessor; for during the battle against the enemies of God he, like a second Moses, "praying in holy purity sends his prayers up to God."

Here is how Eusebius describes the emperor at the moment in which he entered the first Council of Nicaea (325): "Like an angel of God descended from heaven, radiant in the fiery glow of the purple and adorned with gold and precious gems—such was his outward appearance. But his soul was visibly ornamented with the fear and adoration of God." The emperor is described virtually as a superman bearing the marks of divinity "in the manner of his gait and his whole form" which "towered over all his retinue in stature as in brightness of beauty, in majestic dignity and insurpassable strength of body." The scene at the Council of Nicaea, where the bishops sat at table with the emperor, seemed to Eusebius akin to a miracle: "One might easily have thought it a picture of the kingdom of Christ, the whole a dream rather than reality." Another metaphor was most dramatically carried out in the tomb of Constantine, for the emperor was buried in the midst of the sarcophagi of the twelve apostles, six on his right and six on his left. Those sarcophagi contained relics of the apostles, so that Constantine was symbolically flanked by the twelve apostles, and thus almost equated with the Redeemer himself.

This portrait that Eusebius painted of Constantine remained the prototype of the Christian emperor and continued to dominate the historical, political and ecclesiastical mentality of Orthodoxy. The Christian emperor had been made both the political and the sacramental heir of the Roman god-emperor.

Emperor and Patriarch

Once the ruler had been installed in so dominant a position, it was extremely difficult for an independent Church to develop alongside him. From the start the chief bishop of the Church of the Empire was restricted to his spiritual functions: his task was to safeguard doctrinal purity and supervise the modes of divine worship. Nor did the bishop have the latter department all to himself, for the emperor occupied a special place in it. He was the only layman permitted to attend the Eucharist inside the sanctuary, behind the iconostasis. In this respect the emperor enjoyed the same solemn privilege as ordained priests.

The Orthodox theologians called this conjunction of the Christian emperor and the head of the Christian Church a *symphonia,* that is, a concord or harmony. Even the emperor, it must be said, was subordinated to the Church's spiritual guidance, insofar as he was a son of the Church. But in reality the balance of power was very much on the side of the Christian emperor.

In the sixth and seventh centuries the *Epanagoge,* the imperial code of law, permanently fixed this special position of the emperor within the Church. From that time forth there was no chance for independent authority to accrue to the Byzantine patriarch in the manner of the Roman pope. Nevertheless, the Epanagoge did not completely subordinate the patriarch to the emperor; it stated explicitly that the patriarch was to "stand without fear before the emperor for the truth and for the defense of the holy teachings." The patriarch was assured spiritual, if not political, freedom and autonomy. Consequently, Byzantine and Slavic political history do not contain those fateful tensions between Empire and a politicalized Church which characterize the history of the West. There was, however, a struggle between an imperium that attempted to use its political absolutism to curtail the spiritual freedom of the Church, and a Church that fought to maintain spiritual freedom as against absolutistic Caesarism.

2. AUGUSTINE AS THE FATHER OF ROMAN ECCLESIASTICISM AND POLITICAL METAPHYSICS

The Question of Who Was to Blame for the Collapse of the Pagan Empire

Augustine's great treatise on the City of God was written between the years 413 and 426. The memory was still fresh of the times of Theodosius the Great (emperor from 379 to 395), who had enabled the Orthodox Church in the Roman Empire to win a complete victory over paganism and heresy. By the edict of February 28, 380, Theodosius had proclaimed the Catholic faith the religion of the Empire and condemned all deviations from it as punishable heresy. Thanks to his policies, Byzantium, the "New Rome" founded half a century before by Constantine, became truly the respected core of a new *Imperium Christianum*. Under Theodosius, state and Church, emperor and patriarch of Byzantium, were united in a genuine *symphonia*. This same Theodosius had, however, also acknowledged to the world the spiritual power of the Church even over the emperor by publicly doing penance (390) in Bishop Ambrose's church in Milan for having ordered or permitted his Gothic troops to butcher the townspeople of Salonika.

Augustine's book on the City of God was intended as an answer to the most painful question of "guilt" in the fifth century. In 410, Rome herself had been invaded by barbarians; Alaric the Goth had conquered the capital of the ancient pagan Empire and shattered the governmental apparatus. Who was to blame for this almost unbelievable catastrophe? The surviving members of Rome's officialdom and aristocracy, the majority of whom were still pagan, laid the destruction of Rome at the door of the Christians. Had not the Christians for centuries been stubbornly resisting the religious basis of the *Imperium Romanum,* the cult of the emperor? Had they not been undermining the authority of the state and the law, the effectiveness of the army and police? So it was the Christians who were principally responsible for the collapse of the Empire. Augustine undertook to refute this charge.

If we ask ourselves what form of refutation we might expect from a citizen of the great age of the Byzantine Empire, it seems clear that only one argument would do: an invocation of the triumphant glories of New Rome. The old pagan Rome that had persecuted and martyred the Son of God and his saints was gone; its heritage had been transferred to New Rome, to Christian Byzantium, the seat of the Christian emperor, defender of the Christian Church and protector of the Christian religion, guardian of righteousness; to New Rome, the seat of the patriarch who was the image of Christ and teacher of truth.

Augustine Ignores Byzantium

Yet there is not a trace of any such argument in the works of St. Augustine. He ignored the most obvious and fashionable political gambit of his age: the prestige of the New Rome. As far as he was concerned, the Christian Empire did not exist at all. In fact, the western Roman Empire of his age, which was already Christian, appears in his works—at least in the few allusions he makes to it—altogether as if it were still the old pagan Empire, the "devil's state." To Augustine, the great counterpart to the doomed pagan Roman Empire was not Christian Byzantium, but the Catholic Church. This had been created by Christ and was in itself the visible sign, the embodiment and representation upon earth of the kingdom of God.

The question of why Augustine so resolutely ignored the New Rome has scarcely been studied. Nevertheless Augustine's answer to the question of "guilt" turned the ecclesiastical destiny of the Latin West in an entirely new direction, one that led the Church of the West further and further away from the Byzantine Church. In the West a new power took shape: the Roman Church, the Church of the Bishop of Rome. This Church regarded itself as the successor to the vanished *Imperium Romanum*. A political vacuum had been created in the West when the invading Germanic tribes destroyed the Roman administrative apparatus. The Catholic Church stepped into this vacuum and waxed great as the heir to the Roman Empire. It was only under such conditions that the idea of the papacy could develop as it did under such great popes as Gregory I, who as bishops of Rome sought to follow in the footsteps of the vanished emperors.

The Roman Church as
Successor to the Imperium Romanum

Only the political vacuum that followed the Germanic invasions, and only the ideological basis established by Augustine, made possible the legal fiction known as the "Donation of Constantine." The whole story was a retroactive attempt to reconstruct the history of the Roman papacy to make it appear that the newly won political position of the Church was "historical," legitimate and "had always been." The Church produced the forged document, according to which the Emperor Constantine, in gratitude for having been miraculously cured of leprosy by the

Pope's prayers, had given Pope Sylvester I his palace, the insignia of his power, sovereignty over the entire West, and the right to arrange the papal court on the model of the imperial court. Constantine had furthermore transferred his own imperial residence to Byzantium so that the power of the Bishop of Rome would not be diminished by the presence of an emperor in Rome.

This was not only detracting from the nimbus of Byzantium but dispelling it completely and replacing it with a myth of a Christian Rome. The forged document was an attempt to endow the Roman bishop, the new master of Christian Rome, with all the functions of the Roman emperor as that emperor's legal heir. Supposedly the emperor had left behind in Rome all his earthly powers and privileges, adding these to the already existing spiritual powers of the Pope. Now removed to Byzantium, he would continue to attend to his political duties in the East as a faithful son of the Roman Church. But the Bishop of Rome was to live in his palace and wear the triple tiara as a sign that he had also taken over the emperor's crown. Rome herself was to be doubly the center of the Empire, for it housed the single head of both the earthly and the spiritual imperium.

St. Augustine, then, was the fork in the road; henceforth East and West would travel in two different directions. Before long two totally different types of Christian conception of Church and state had grown up. It is not surprising that the end was to be schism between Byzantium and Rome. The emperors and patriarchs of Byzantium could no more follow the Roman popes along the road of evolving papal primacy than the Roman popes could pay homage to the myth of Byzantium as the "New Rome"— since the papal supremacy rested upon the claim that the *Imperium Romanum* had been reborn, as the Christian City of God, in the Roman Church. An ideology of this sort could only have arisen in the political vacuum resulting from the collapse of the Empire in the West. The Roman emperor had deserted Rome for Byzantium, so that there was no longer any secular ruler in Rome to check the growing power and pride of the Church.

3. FURTHER EVOLUTION
OF THE BYZANTINE SYSTEM
AMONG THE EASTERN SLAVS

But in the Byzantine Empire, the head of the Church could scarcely presume to lay any claim to political and legal authority beyond his spiritual authority within the *Imperium Christianum*. The Christian emperor was on the spot keeping sharp watch over his rights and quick to curb any pretensions to ecclesiastical primacy. A *symphonia* had indeed been established, and friction arose only where the emperor himself violated the moral law or the doctrines of the Church. At that point the head of the Church could invoke his spiritual privileges to reprove the emperor and, should he remain obstinately impenitent or heretical, employ the Church's disciplinary methods against him. Open conflict between the emperor and the metropolitan or patriarch developed only in such a situation—for example, in the struggle between Ivan IV, the Terrible and Metropolitan Filipp (1507–69).

The special danger within the system lay not in a possible assumption of political power by the head of the Church, but vice versa—the emperor might abuse his position within this state-Church system to decrease the inner freedom of the Church and reduce the Church completely to a tool of the state. This took place at several periods in both Byzantine and Russian history.

The political ideology of Russian tsarism was rooted directly in the Byzantine conception of Church and state as this had been formulated by Emperor Constantine. The East Slavs took over the idea of the Christian state and the Christian Caesar in whom were merged the qualities of the Greek philosopher-king, the Christian monarch and the anointed of the Lord. Constantine had made himself the head of the Byzantine state Church and each of his successors was felt to be the vicar of God upon earth. From the very beginning this same conception was implicit in the Russian Empire.

However it was only after the fall of Byzantium that this Byzantine ideology was fully elaborated and merged into the awakening national consciousness of Muscovy. The Grand Duchy of Moscow henceforth claimed to the full the religious heritage of the shattered second Rome. The premise that Moscow was the third Rome became the basis for the Muscovite state Church (see p. 179).

The specifically Muscovite ideology known as Yossifinism grew out of the doctrines of Yossif Sanin (1439–1515), abbot of Volokalamsk Monastery. Dominion over state and Church, so the argument ran, lay in the hand of the tsar, the divinely anointed vicar of God. That part of Russian monasticism which resolutely guarded the spiritual freedom of the Church was strongly opposed to the doctrine and waged a tenacious struggle against it. Though Yossifinism was very much in keeping with the fundamental ideas of the Byzantine state Church it represented a further step in aggrandizement of the tsar. As the Christian autocrat, he was granted an increase in his spiritual as well as his temporal powers, with the result that the metropolitans, and later the patriarchs, were shorn of any authority over him.

4. DIFFERENCE BETWEEN THE BYZANTINE AND THE MUSCOVITE SYSTEM

This special evolution may in part be explained by the difference in age between the two states. In the Byzantine Empire, Church and state had skirmished with one another for many centuries. Out of innumerable minor frays fought with spiritual and political weapons there had emerged a curious harmony. The two powers had adapted to one another and had created a certain tradition of respect for each other's limits and rights. There was no time for anything of the sort in Muscovy. Russia was a young nation, created by the ambitions of tempestuous dukes. From the first the secular rulers had usurped significant powers over ecclesiastical affairs.

Ivan the Terrible (1530–84) made it plain that the Church could not exercise even the last remnant of spiritual freedom: the right to reprove the tsar if he openly violated ecclesiastical morals and discipline. Yossifinism had so strengthened the hegemony of the tsar that the Church became helpless even in this last resort. Thus Byzantine "harmony" between state and Church was shattered. A form of national Russian Caesaropapism came into being, in what might be called a rightist deviation from the original status of the Orthodox Church.

The reform attempted by Patriarch Nikon from 1652 to 1667 looked to restoration of the original Byzantine relationship. But Nikon was also departing from the Byzantine model. In opposing tsarism's excessive authority over the Church, he demanded a number of secular rights in addition to his spiritual powers. Nikon's claim to complete independence of the Church as against the state represented, so to speak, the leftist deviation from the Byzantine tradition. Nikon failed completely and was deposed. His deposition was followed by still more rigorous repression and abridgment of the spiritual freedom of the Church, and the complete triumph of Yossifinism.

5. PETER THE GREAT

After all this it was an easy matter for Peter the Great in the Age of Enlightenment to apply the principles of absolutism to his relations with the Church. He regarded himself as sovereign lord of the Church with the right to reshape the structure of the Russian Orthodox Church to suit himself. He abolished the patriarchal organization and established the government of the Church on a synodal basis, along lines suggested by Samuel von Pufendorf, the German Lutheran. His qualms at tampering with time-honored institutions were all the fewer because he no longer felt any strong personal ties with Orthodoxy. His reign signalized the snuffing out of the last vestiges of freedom and autonomy possessed by the Russian Orthodox Church. With the abolition of the patriarchal organization, the Church was placed under the supervision of a secular procurator.

XI.

Rome, Byzantium, Moscow

1. BYZANTIUM AND ROME

Byzantium, the "New Rome"

The relationship of Byzantium and Rome has generally been regarded from the Western or Roman Catholic point of view. Seen thus, Byzantium appears as the metropolis of the Eastern Roman Empire which, intent on rivaling Rome, refused to be subordinate to her in doctrinal matters, struck out in new directions, and ultimately parted altogether from the Roman creed. This picture is a typically Western historical myth colored by dogma. It will be instructive for once to compare the relationship of Byzantium and Rome from the Byzantine point of view. Throughout the Byzantine Empire, Constantinople was proudly called New Rome, while Byzantine citizens were referred to as *Rômaioi*—Romans. As the Byzantines themselves understood their historical role, Byzantium was the direct continuation, decreed in God's plan for the universe, of Roman history. In calling themselves *Rômaioi* the Byzantines underlined their emperor's legal claim to Rome's onetime universal dominion. In speaking of New

Rome they implied both the continuity and the difference. New Rome was entitled to all the powers of old Rome, but at the same time she was Christian Rome and exercised the might of the Roman Empire according to the law of Christ.

It cannot be determined with certainty whether Emperor Constantine himself used the term "New Rome" in referring to the city he was founding. We do know that he wished to build "the second Rome," that is to say, a second capital of the Empire; that he established a Senate in Constantinople, transplanted a number of the leading families of Rome to the new capital, and that he laid out Constantinople as far as possible according to the city plan of Rome. In any case, "the second Rome" very rapidly became a "New Rome." For old Rome was conquered by the Germans and thenceforth was drawn into the political maelstrom that produced such chaotic conditions throughout Italy and the whole of the West during the great migrations. Old Rome ceased to be a political and administrative center. Byzantium took its place. In 381 the Council of Constantinople officially confirmed New Rome as the name for Byzantium.

"Renovatio"

After the collapse of the western half of the Empire, a new ideology began to make rapid headway in Byzantium. It was no longer enough to say that the new Rome was the equal of the old; the feeling was that the new Rome took precedence over the old. The collapse of Rome was explained as the rightful vengeance of God upon the metropolis of the pagan Empire which for so many centuries had persecuted the Christian Church. From the sixth century onward, we can see the unfolding of the idea of *renovatio* in Byzantium. The idea reached its zenith in the heroic twelfth century of the Eastern Empire. Byzantium, according to this version of history, was a young and vital Rome in contrast to the aging and decrepit Rome of the

West. The verse chronicle of Manasses, composed during the reign of Manuel Comnenus, describes the plundering of Rome by Genseric the Vandal in 455 and concludes: "This happened to old Rome; but our Rome flourishes, grows, is vigorous and young; may it grow forever, O Lord, Ruler of the world, since it has such an emperor."

Defection of Rome from Byzantium

Two other important factors helped to precipitate the separation of New Rome from old Rome. 1) During the period of chaos that began with the invasions the Roman popes profited by the absence of the emperor to extend their ecclesiastical dominion and gain political leadership in the West. They more and more defied the overlordship of the Byzantine emperors by, for example, resisting the collection of imperial taxes and hindering the exercise of other imperial rights on Roman soil. Byzantium regarded this conduct as open rebellion and reproached the spiritual head of Rome for misusing the woes of the times to increase his own power at the expense of Empire. 2) It was a fresh affront to Byzantium when the Pope entered a political coalition with the enemies of the Empire, namely the rulers of the Frankish kingdom, and went so far as to confer the imperial title upon a barbarian German king—Charlemagne—while a legitimate Roman emperor still occupied the imperial throne in Byzantium. As Byzantium saw it, the Bishop of Rome and the Western barbarian kings were distributing powers and titles they had no legitimate right to. At this point the Byzantine idea of *renovatio* was carried further and merged into the idea of the *translatio imperii,* the transference of the Empire from old to New Rome. Even as the West began to comport itself as a new Holy Roman Empire, the Byzantines asserted that Constantine had transferred the entire Senate and the entire official hierarchy of Rome to Constantinople and that nothing of the imperium was left to Rome after the foundation of Constantinople.

Dispute over the Primacy

In keeping with this political conception, the Byzantine Church arrived at its own version of the *translatio* idea. Until the ninth century it held firm to its acknowledged equality with the Roman see. Patriarch Photius (858–67 and 877–86) was the first to put forth the claim of primacy for Constantinople. He defended his new pretensions on the ground that the Bishop of Rome had become an apostate; he had departed from the true faith, had proved unworthy of his honors, and had therefore lost his right to the see of Constantinople. As further support, Photius adduced the same forged document with which the Roman papacy had backed its own claim to primacy: the Donation of Constantine (see p. 169). Since the document spoke of Constantine's having taken with him to Constantinople the whole Senate and officialdom of Rome, the Byzantines could use it to corroborate their assertion that nothing pertaining to the imperium had been left behind in old Rome. And since the Bishop of Rome himself had meanwhile become a heretic, the Church of Constantinople, on the basis of the canon of the Council of Chalcedon, was the proper heir of the rights of the Roman Church. Princess Anna Comnena in the twelfth century expressed this theory in bold phraseology: "After the secular rule of Rome had been transferred to our imperial city, and the whole Senate and official hierarchy with it, the position of the bishops as archpresbyters was naturally transferred to this city also."

There was still one logical stumbling block: the Roman boast that the Apostle Peter had founded the Church in Rome. To offset this historical argument, the Byzantine Church fetched up the legend of the Apostle Andrew. From the time of Patriarch Photius, the Byzantine Church made much of the fact that it had been founded by Andrew. And since Andrew had been called by the Savior before

Peter, it was clear that the Byzantine Church had an older lineage than the Roman.

Alienation

By such avenues did old and new Rome arrive at a point where each of the partners was eager to deny the legality of the other's claims to ecclesiastical and political leadership, where each charged the other with defection from the true faith, where the sense of fraternity of the Christian churches was abolished and finally where each was pitted against the other in the field of war. In the course of those great adventures in foreign policy called the Crusades, the West was offered the chance to conquer and crush Byzantium. The opportunity was not renounced: in 1204 Constantinople was captured by the warriors of the Fourth Crusade, who linked it to the Latin Empire and tried to set up the Latin patriarchate of Constantinople. As we have already seen, this subjugation by the Latin West, and the subsequent persecution of the Orthodox Church, immeasurably deepened the existing schism and gave an almost traumatic character to Byzantine Orthodoxy's antagonism toward Rome.

2. MOSCOW AND ROME

Moscow, the "Third Rome"

In 1453 the new Rome on the Bosporus fell into the hands of the Turks. But the end of the Byzantine Empire did not extinguish the Byzantine tradition. Rather, its ideas and its claims were taken over by the Russian rulers of Moscow. The Russian historical and ecclesiastical mentality grew out of the conception of Moscow as the "third Rome." The Muslim conquest of Constantinople had not only wiped out the last focus of power in the Byzantine Empire, it had also destroyed the real heart of the Eastern Church: *Hagia Sophia,* the holiest cathedral of the Church. This spiritual and liturgical center of the Eastern Orthodox

Church was converted into a mosque. Henceforth the Grand Duchy of Moscow was the last remaining politically independent Orthodox power. The conquest of Constantinople affected Muscovy's conception of her historical and ecclesiastical mission in much the same way as the conquest of Rome by the Germanic tribes had affected Byzantium's view of herself. Russian national and ecclesiastical pride received an enormous impetus from the notion that Moscow had become the "third Rome." After the collapse of the Byzantine Empire and Church, the political claims of the Roman *Imperium* and the spiritual claims of the Byzantine Church were assumed by Muscovy and the Church of Moscow.

The Transfer of the Imperial Eagle from Byzantium to Moscow

During the two centuries preceding the fall of Constantinople both the spiritual and the temporal powers had been subjected to frequent severe crises. The new Slav states made various attempts to take over the historical role of Byzantium. As early as the tenth century the Bulgarian ruler Simeon (893–927) was already assuming the Byzantine title, styling himself "Emperor and Autocrat of all the Bulgars and Greeks." This could scarcely be tolerated and the first Bulgarian Empire was destroyed by Byzantium; but after its restoration in 1185 we find Ivan Asen I assuming the title of "Tsar and Autocrat of the Bulgars in Christ." In 1349, Prince Stevan Dushan of Serbia assumed the title of Caesar (Tsar), claiming that he was historical successor to the rulers of Constantinople. The fall of the imperial city itself greatly furthered this idea of inherited Caesarship on the soil of the Grand Duchy of Moscow. The idea was further promoted by the marriage of Grand Duke Ivan III (1462–1505) to the Byzantine princess Sophia. Ivan III zealously fostered the concept of the third Rome. It was he who introduced the two-headed Byzantine eagle into the Russian state insignia and made the title "Tsar of all Russia" a reality.

The Russian Tsar—the "New Constantine"

Precisely at this time the Church became convinced that it stood at the beginning of a new age. According to its computations, the year 1492 marked the end of the seventh and last millennium of the world's history. The Last Days which had been promised in the Apocalypse were approaching. The Moscow Church counted on the end with such conviction that it did not continue its calendar beyond 1492. The world should and must come to an end at the end of the seventh millennium. Had there not been only seven councils? Were there not only seven days to the week, seven sacraments, and seven pillars of wisdom?

But the world did not end, and Metropolitan Zosimus had to have new Easter tables made. In the preface accompanying their publication he heralded the dawn of a new Christian era. He further ordained that God had now chosen, after St. Vladimir, the "devout Ivan Vasilievich as Tsar and Autocrat of all Russia" to be a new Emperor Constantine for a new Constantinople, namely Moscow. At the beginning of the world's eighth millennium the Grand Duke of Moscow stood proclaimed by the highest dignitary of the Russian Church as the protector of Orthodoxy, and the direct descendant of the devout Emperor Constantine.

The Letters of Filofey

The new ideology was most distinctly put forth in the letters of Starets Filofey of Pskov (†1547) directed to the ruler of Moscow. In one he wrote: "I should like to say a few words about the existing Orthodox realm of our ruler. He is upon earth the only Tsar over the Christians, the leader of the Apostolic Church that stands now in the blessed city of Moscow instead of Rome and Constantinople. It alone glows brighter than the sun throughout the world; for know, thou devout one, that all Christian realms have run their course and all together have passed over into the realm of our ruler, in keeping with the prophetic books. Such is the Russian Empire. For two empires have fallen, but the third stands, and there will be no fourth. . . . The woman clothed with the sun, with the moon under her feet, and on her head a crown of twelve stars, the Christian Church of whom John speaks, who fled from the dragon into the wilderness—she fled from old Rome because of *azyme*[1]; great Rome fell because of the Apollinarian heresy. The woman fled to the new Rome; that is the city of Constantine. But there too she found no rest, for they had united with the Latins, at the eighth Council. The Church of Constantinople was destroyed. But she fled to the third Rome, which is new, great Russia. Now, being the only Apostolic Church, she shines more brightly than the sun in all the world, and the great and devout Russian Tsar alone leads and preserves her. Let him be on guard and be watchful, by the grace and wisdom of our Lord."

It is significant that the historical theory herein expressed, the transference of the Empire from Byzantium to Moscow, is justified on grounds of apostasy, just as the claim of Byzantium to being the "New Rome" was similarly justified. Byzantium charged that Rome had lost her precedence by falling into heresy; here the destruction of Byzantium is regarded as divine retribution for the Latin heresy, that is the union with Rome. The fact that Byzantium had entered into negotiation with Rome because of the military pressure of the Turks was not, in Moscow, considered sufficient extenuation. Rome herself was the quintessence of heresy; therefore, to make common cause with her was heresy. The Russian conception of both Church and state was formed in terms of this ideology of "the third Rome."

[1] *azyme* (Gk.) = unleavened bread. The Orthodox used leavened bread for the Eucharist and regarded the unleavened bread used in Rome as unseemly.

According to this doctrine, Russian tsarism and the Russian Orthodox Church merged. The "great and devout" Tsar Ivan IV, upon his coronation in the Cathedral of the Ascension in Moscow, assumed the title of "Holy Tsar and Autocrat of all Russia, crowned by God." Inspired by this idea, in which a sense of religious, ecclesiastical and political destinies were inextricably interwoven, Ivan IV set out to expand the Russian Empire.

The Patriarchate of Moscow

It was in the same spirit that the Russian Church requested and obtained a patriarchate of its own. In 1588, when Patriarch Jeremias II of Constantinople paid a visit to Moscow, Boris Godunov persuaded him to establish an independent Russian patriarchate. On January 26, 1589, Metropolitan Job was solemnly consecrated "Patriarch of Moscow and of all Russia." Thus the Moscow Church at last attained the rank that seemed commensurate with its belief in its historic mission.

Armed with this religious idea the Russian patriarchate was able to survive through the gravest crises. It withstood formal abolition and the establishment of a synodal constitution under a government procurator by Peter the Great. When tsarism collapsed under the impact of the Revolution of 1917, the Russian Church, despite the confusions of the period and the onset of severe persecution by the Bolshevists, took courage and reinstituted its patriarchate. Despite the violent opposition of the Bolshevist regime to the principle of the patriarchate and its antipathy to the first holder of the dignity under the Revolution, Patriarch Tikhon, the Church stood firm and preserved this form of organization.

XII.

Russia and Europe

Does Russia Belong to Asia or to Europe?

Under the stress of current political problems, there is a tendency to look at Russia and see all the ways in which her intellectual, political and social structures are at variance with those of Europe. In short, Russia is consigned to "Asia." This political myth draws its sustenance from the idea of an eternal threat to Europe by "Asia." It is rather fashionable to compare Soviet Russia's present threat to Europe to the Mongol invasions of the Middle Ages. An epigram embodying this myth was, in fact, already coined in the nineteenth century: *"Grattez le Russe et vous trouvez le Tatare."* People will also point to the special ecclesiastical development of Russia, her choice of the Byzantine form of Christianity, as another example of her "Asiatic" character. We cannot therefore give an account of the Orthodox Church without considering this question. From the historian's point of view we can only say that the idea of Russia as an "Asian" country is pure shibboleth. A quick survey of the religious and ecclesiastical history of Russia makes this amply clear.

1. RUSSIA AS PART OF EUROPE

The Duchy of Kiev

From the days of the old Duchy of Kiev, Russia had always been objectively an integral part of Europe and of European history. Subjectively, too, she felt herself linked to Europe. The princes of Rus had been allied by marriage to the most important of the Scandinavian and German princely families. The Duchy of Kiev itself maintained the closest political, cultural and economic ties with its neighbors to the north and west. A feeling of separation from the Church of the West had not yet sprung up. Especially close ecclesiastical ties existed between Kiev and Prague, so much so that St. Wenceslas was one of the most revered of saints in the Duchy of Kiev, and his legend was translated into Old Church Slavonic.

During the Turkish wars of the seventeenth and eighteenth centuries Poland was called the "bulwark of Christendom"—*antemurale Christianitatis propugnaculum Ecclesiae*. The same term might well be applied to the Duchy of Kiev for earlier centuries. Christian Kiev was engaged in constant struggles with the Khazar, the Petcheneg, the Cuman, and the Bulgar tribes. Within a few decades of its Christianization, Kiev assumed the military and spiritual task that had been the lot of Byzantium in Asia Minor ever since the fourth century. At the cost of great sacrifices, she constituted herself Christendom's bulwark against the ever-renewed assaults of Asiatic nomads. In this respect Kiev was carrying out a task that paralleled that of the Merovingian kingdom in the West, when it succeeded in stemming the Arab invasions from the Iberian Peninsula.

Muscovy "Bulwark of Christendom"

The same assignment was later taken over from Kiev by the Duchy of Moscow. To be sure, the Mongol invasion destroyed Kiev; the Russian dukes became vassals of the

Mongol khans. But since, as we have seen, the Mongol rulers followed the principles of the "Great Yasa" and tolerated all religions, the Orthodox Church lost none of its possessions and rights in the Russian duchies occupied by the Mongols. The Russian Orthodox Church could continue as the real heart of a national Russian culture throughout the period in which the Russian duchies had been stripped of their political sovereignty. A similar phenomenon may be seen in the Orthodox churches of Greece and Serbia during the period of Turkish dominion in the Balkans, or in the Orthodox Church of Cyprus under present-day British occupation. These churches became the center of the national and cultural self-consciousness of their peoples and provided the intellectual basis for their liberation movements. Indeed, the freedom fighters often gathered around their bishop's ecclesiastical banner. So, too, the Orthodox Church in Russia became, during the Tatar era, the principal nucleus for the intellectual and later the political resistance to the Mongol overlords. The first military efforts to shake off the Mongol yoke were undertaken as an Orthodox crusade against the Mongol unbelievers. The leader of this crusade was Ivan the Terrible, who took advantage of the dissension among the various Mongol chiefs and called together Russian forces in the name of the holy cause of Orthodoxy.

Leibnitz's View of Russia

Central and western Europe never forgot that Muscovy belonged to the *corpus Christianum*. Evidence of this may be found in the various political programs Leibnitz presented to the monarchs of his age. In a youthful essay written in 1669 he treated the Grand Duke of Moscow from the Polish and Roman Catholic point of view as the "Turk of the North"; but in the memorial on European politics which he wrote in August 1670, entitled *Considerations on the Security of the German Empire*, he viewed the Grand Duchy of Moscow as "a possible future

ally" of the European powers for their common defensive
struggle against the Turks and Tatars.

The same ideas were further explored in the *Consilium
Aegyptiacum*, a study that Leibnitz wrote for Louis XIV,
in which he pointed out all the advantages to be derived
from the Holy Roman emperor's marching with the Poles
and Swedes against the Turks while the Russians attacked
the Tatars, who were constantly disturbing the empire from
their base in Kherson. The sensible thing for Russia to do
was to exterminate these robbers rather than to advance
against the West and occupy Riga. In letters and memorials
addressed to Peter the Great, Leibnitz hammered away
at this idea. Peter the Great was so impressed by this advice
that he conferred the title of a Russian King's Counsel upon
the German philosopher. Again and again Leibnitz pointed
out to the tsar that the most important task of a Christian
monarch was war against the Turks. The tsar's journey to
central Europe encouraged the philosopher to hatch broad
political programs; he hoped to bring about an alliance of
Poland, Russia and the empire which would drive the
archfoe of Christendom, the Turks, from European soil.
In all this political speculation Leibnitz took it for granted
that the Grand Duchy of Moscow was an integral part of
European Christendom.

Russia as the Savior of Europe in the Napoleonic Wars.
The Holy Alliance

During the dramatic years of the Napoleonic wars the
belief arose on Russian soil that the Russian Empire was
not just an ordinary part of Europe, but the godsent, destined savior of Europe. Tsar Alexander I enthusiastically
promoted the conception of the Holy Alliance: the three
great rulers of Europe, who also represented the three great
Christian confessions (Orthodox Russia under Alexander I, Protestant Prussia under Frederick William III and
Catholic Austria under Francis I) were uniting to save
Europe from the Antichrist who threatened them from the

West. The allegory was borne out by the eventual victory of the Russian army over Napoleon, a redemption that was purchased at the price of burning "Holy" Moscow.

The Burning of Moscow

From the very start the Russian people injected religious meaning into the War of 1812. The burning of Moscow seemed to them a great self-immolation Holy Russia was making in behalf of all Europe in order to break the power of the hitherto invincible Antichrist. At a time of deep misfortune the people saw in the burning of Moscow the manifestation of God's saving mercy. This religious note is likewise sounded in Tsar Alexander's proclamation of thanksgiving: "He who guides the destinies of nations, Almighty God, has chosen the venerable capital of Russia to save, through her sufferings, not Russia alone, but all of Europe. Her fire was the conflagration of freedom for all the kingdoms of the earth. Out of the offences against her Holy Church sprang the victory of Faith. The Kremlin, undermined by evil, crushed in its fall the chief of the evil-doers." In similar terms Alexander addressed Bishop Eilert, a Protestant, in Berlin: "The burning of Moscow has illuminated my soul. The judgment of the Lord upon the ice-covered fields has filled my heart with the warmth of Faith. . . . Now I am coming to know God. Since that time I have been a changed man. I owe my own redemption and liberation to the salvation of Europe from ruin."

The sense of belonging to Europe was, it is clear, founded upon the idea of an ecumenical unity of the Christian confessions and kingdoms of Europe. This ecumenical idea meant that the Russians had overcome their centuries-long dislike and mistrust of Rome which had been bred by the Crusades. France, once the principal power of Europe and now revolutionary and atheistic, was manifesting itself as the great betrayer of the idea of a Christian Europe, whereas Russia had emerged as the instrument chosen by God to save European Christendom.

The Slavophiles

Those theoreticians who treasure the idea of an unbridge-able gulf existing between Russia and Europe are fond of citing the historical views and cultural philosophy of the Slavophiles. Here were representative figures of Russian Orthodoxy, they point out, who themselves were of the opinion that such a gulf existed between Russia and the "rotten West." It is true that a large number of quotations can be garnered from the writings of Ivan Kireevsky, Constantine and Ivan Aksakov and Yury Samarin, in which much is made of the contrasts between Russia and the West, these contrasts being attributed to the Orthodox character of Russia. They repeat the stereotyped claim that Russia is the carrier of Orthodox "truth" (*pravda*), and argue that the inner degeneracy of the West is due to Roman Catholicism.

We should not be misled, however, into seeing these Slavophile doctrines as proof of a real dichotomy between Russia and Europe. Interestingly enough, the Slavophiles set forth their criticisms of the West in a periodical called *The European,* which Ivan Kireevsky began publishing in 1832. Even the most radical of the Slavophiles did not consider the "rotten West" to be synonymous with Europe, nor were they suggesting that Russia ought to exclude herself from Europe. The origin and descent of their ideas are highly significant. The ideology of the Slavophiles was rooted most strongly in German romanticism and in German idealistic philosophy, chiefly the philosophies of Hegel, Schelling and Franz von Baader. It can be traced further back to the ideas of Herder. In its themes and its viewpoint, Slavophile theory moved completely within a European framework.

The Slavophiles were, in fact, one more of those groups of romantic intellectuals who emerged in various European countries during the nineteenth century, most conspicuously in Germany. Their nationalism too was a specifically romantic trait, and even the messianism generally considered so characteristic of the Slavophiles displayed features that could be found among other romantic groups in various countries of Europe. Thus the Slavophiles scarcely serve as "proof" that Russia belongs to Asia rather than Europe. They actually show that the intellectual, religious and philosophical development of Russia was consistent with the general development of Europe. Russian Slavophilism with its offshoots of nationalism and messianism represents only a variant of the romantic nationalism of Germany or England. The Slavophiles' criticism of the "rotten West" was for the most part identical, even to details, with German romanticists' criticism of the French Enlightenment, of aspects of the French Revolution, and of the first glimmerings of modern technical and materialistic thinking. Yet no historian would ever dream of calling German romanticism an Asiatic phenomenon.

Nor did the Russian Slavophiles ever carry their polemics against the West to the point of assigning Russia and themselves to Asia rather than Europe. For them too Russia always remained a part of the Christian European world. And although they distinguished Russia, as the "East," from the "Latinism" of the West, Russia remained in their eyes "Western" and "European" in relation to Asia. This is true above all for Dostoevsky, who never ceased to refer to himself as a "Russian European," and who repeatedly declared: "We cannot give up Europe." "Only the Russian, even in our time, which is to say, long before the general balance has been drawn up, only the Russian has been given the capacity to be most Russian when he is most European."

The Crimean War as "Europe's Betrayal of Russia"

The Crimean War severely shook Russia's sense of fellowship with Europe. This intellectual crisis was, however, brought about not by Russia, but by Catholic circles in France. There was a significant difference between the German and the French attitudes toward Russia during the Crimean War. Prussia felt that at bottom she was still linked with Russia by the Holy Alliance. In the debates on the Crimean War held in the Prussian parliament, Friedrich Julius Stahl, the conservative theologian and student of canon law, insisted that the Holy Alliance was nothing but the modern continuation of the old idea of the Roman Empire and of the Christian solidarity of the nations included within that Empire. This tells us something of the extent to which Russia was regarded by the Prussians as a natural member of the Christian and European community of nations.

France took an altogether different view. France's participation in the Crimean War was expressly sanctioned by the Archbishop of Paris. In a pastoral letter he described the war as a crusade against the "heresy of Photius." He was reviving the ancient anti-Orthodox position of the Roman Catholic West, for during the Middle Ages the Roman Catholic Church had proclaimed the struggle against Byzantium to be one branch of the crusade against Islam. No wonder that the Russians felt that the West was banding against her and no wonder the Slavophiles denounced France and England for betraying her.

Yet not even this experience could extinguish the Russian sense of belonging to Christian Europe. That is plainly to be seen in the work of so distinguished a thinker as Vladimir Soloviev. One of Soloviev's favorite ideas was that the Christian world could only resist the onslaught of non-Christian Asia if it clung to the ideal of its ecumenical unity. If the Christian world, including Russia, were ever to turn away from this idea, he contended, the non-Christian Far East would inevitably bring about the downfall of Europe. If the Occident forgot its mission as the pillar of Christian culture, it would succumb to Asia. In Soloviev's eschatology, the bankruptcy of the Occident was bound up with the end of history. In his famous *Three Conversations*[1] written in 1899–1900, he painted a picture of

[1] Published in English as *War and Christianity: From the Russian Point of View. Three Conversations.* New York, G. P. Putnam's Sons, 1915.

the last war in history, which he predicted would take
place in the twentieth century: the struggle of Europe
against a pagan Asia united under the banner of pan-
Mongolism. In this vision of the future, France was pic-
tured as the betrayer of Christian solidarity—bearing out
Russia's interpretation of the French attitude in the Crimean War. Soloviev envisioned France as joining in an
alliance with the Mongol invaders to save her own skin,
and so furthering the Mongols' rapid conquest of the rest
of Europe.

Russia's sense of being the bulwark of Europe awoke
once more in a new fashion, in what we may call a final,
wholly secularized form, at the time of the Russo-Japanese
War. Once more Russia saw herself as the representative
of Europe opposing the political power of rising Asia, the
"yellow peril" as embodied in Japan. The Russians felt
this all the more keenly because Russia was abandoned by
the European powers in this struggle; they saw themselves
betrayed and ridiculed and took their defeat in the war as
an ominous sign of future victories of the Asiatics over
Europe.

A feeling of genuine solidarity with Christian Europe
has been present throughout Russian history. It has not
just cropped up occasionally as a passing fad, but has been
actively present as a creative intellectual and political
principle. There have been, however, a number of coun-
terforces to this sense of solidarity with Europe, and these
forces have produced an ambivalent attitude toward
Europe.

2. DIVIDING FACTORS

Rome's Battle against the Slavic Liturgy

At the time of the emergence of the Duchy of Kiev, the
fact of a schism between Byzantium and Rome had not yet
penetrated the minds of Russian Christians. The first real
alienation only came about as a result of serious conflicts

with Rome on matters of principle. One such was Rome's antagonism (touched on earlier) to all efforts to introduce a Slavic liturgy among the West Slavic peoples who belonged to the Roman Catholic Church. Policies of this sort seemed to confirm traditional prejudices against Rome and intensified the Kiev Church's dislike for her Western partner.

The Crusades

Above all else the Crusades administered a violent shock to Russian relations with the Latin West. For the first time the East realized how far the Roman papacy had moved from the idea of universal spiritual dominion to a claim of universal political dominion. For here it was mustering its might against the Orthodox Church of the East only because the Eastern Church contested this claim. The fact was that Roman Catholic Christendom's great exploit in foreign policy, which we call the Crusades, operated along the entire eastern front from Scandinavia to Palestine and Egypt, not only as an assault upon the Islamic kingdoms but also as an assault upon the Orthodox Church and Orthodox countries of the East. This episode had the most terrible repercussions for the whole of European history. As a result of the Crusades the Orthodox peoples of the East were alienated and cut off, against their will and against their ancient traditions, from western Europe.

Of still graver import was the fact that the Western offensive hindered the Orthodox states of the East from carrying out the task so vital to all of Europe. That task was to hold off from Europe the non-Christian nomadic peoples of Asia who were advancing with ever increasing strength, or else to force these tribes to settle down under the sway of Christian rulers. The power of the Byzantine Empire was broken before the Turks' capture of Constantinople in 1453. It had been shattered when the Catholic armies of the Fourth Crusade first took Constantinople in 1204. With the establishment of the Latin Empire and

patriarchate in Constantinople and the suppression of Orthodoxy in the Byzantine lands overrun by the Latin con-
querors, the Greek emperor and the Greek patriarch were
forced to take flight to Asia Minor. For half a century both
continued to rule in a remnant of the former Byzantine
Empire. During this period the military and economic
resources of the Empire were totally disorganized, so that
even after the expulsion of the Latins from Byzantium the
emperors were unable to restore the Empire's former
power. By conquering the Byzantine Empire the Latin
West destroyed the strongest bulwark of European Christendom. The "Crusade" waged in the interests of Rome
eliminated the one Christian power in the East which had
hitherto been able to stave off the non-Christian Asiatics
pressing forward from the East.

While the attack on Byzantium made the Eastern Slavs
more inclined to be suspicious of the Latins, they themselves
were not directly affected. But suspicion turned to hatred
when the Catholic Knights of the Teutonic Order, who had
hitherto been crusading against the pagan tribes of the
Baltic region, launched an attack upon the Orthodox
duchies in northern Russia, threatening them from the
West at the same time that the mounted armies of Mongols were harassing them from the East. The Russian
duchies found themselves involved in an apparently hope-
less war on two fronts. This feint on the part of western
Europe intensified their bitterness and their hatred for
Rome (see p. 117 ff.).

The Effects of the Tatar Occupation

For more than three centuries the Russian duchies were
vassal states of the Mongol Empire, a circumstance that
contributed to further alienation of Russia from central and
western Europe. However, the importance of this matter
has been frequently exaggerated. Western historiography
has fostered an exaggerated conception of the racial
changes among the Eastern Slavs produced by the ad-

mixture of Tatar blood. In reality the Tatar admixture among the Russian people at that time was insignificant since the Tatars left no sizable contingents of occupation troops in the Russian duchies. After quick, successful incursions, their mounted armies withdrew, leaving the conquered land in charge of Russian vassal dukes. For the most part they maintained contact with these vassals only through small embassies. Thus there was little mingling of blood. The number of "occupation children" was far less than the "normal" percentage that armies of occupation in all ages have left behind in countries they occupy for any length of time. However, some Russian noble families made political marriages with the daughters of Mongol princes, with the result that the small percentage of Mongol blood was greater in the Russian aristocracy than among the common people.

Nevertheless, political adherence to the Mongol Empire did result in a turning away from western Europe. The diplomatic intercourse, the marriages, the regular exchange of embassies of the Russian duchies with the neighboring duchies of the West Slavs, and with Scandinavia and Germany was discontinued. The formidable tribute that the Mongol khans extracted from the Russian duchies also choked off the economic relations between the Russian duchies and their neighbors to the west. Moreover, the crusaders, by occupying the islands from Malta to Cyprus, had reopened Mediterranean trade, hitherto paralyzed by the Saracens. Italian ports could once again trade with the Levant. Asiatic goods, which had hitherto found their way to the Hanse cities of the Baltic by way of Novgorod, could once more pour into western Europe by way of the Mediterranean. In addition, the integration of the Russian duchies in the administrative apparatus of the Mongol Empire brought about certain changes in the governmental practices of these duchies. These changes represented a break with the previous traditions, which had more or less followed the pattern of medieval European feudalism.

"The Time of Troubles"

Suspicion of the West was further reinforced in the "Time of Troubles" preceding the election of the first Romanov, Tsar Michael. During this period Poland made repeated efforts to win control of the Moscow Duchy. These fresh invasions from the West seemed to the Russians a continuation of the Crusades, for one of the professed aims of the Polish invaders was subjugation of the Russian Orthodox Church to the leadership of Rome. To the Russians the Poles were worse foes than the Tatars —the Tatars, after all, had never interfered with the Orthodox Church, whereas in all the upheavals stirred up and nursed by the Poles during the Time of Troubles, hostility to Orthodoxy was a crucial element.

For these and many other reasons which we cannot here particularize, Russia developed her curiously ambivalent attitude toward western Europe. On the one hand prerevolutionary Russia was conscious of her solidarity with Christian Europe as against the non-Christian powers of Asia—a solidarity that might also be manifested in the contest against anti-Christian revolutionary forces arising in western Europe itself and seeking to overthrow the traditional Christian social order, as was the case during the Napoleonic wars. On the other hand there arose a sense of profound difference between Orthodox Russia and the Roman Catholic West; wariness was intensified into a highly idiosyncratic mingling of hatred and love. But even during periods of her most intense aloofness from the Roman Catholic or the Protestant West, Russia never cast her lot with Asia. On the contrary, she regarded the attitudes of the European powers toward her quarrels with Turkey in the Crimean War and with Japan in the Russo-Japanese War as betrayals. In the last analysis, Russia believed in European solidarity. Nothing in her ecclesiastical and religious history accords with the popular theory that Russia belongs to Asia.

XIII.

Orthodoxy within the Universal Church Today

The Position of Orthodoxy within the Ecumenical Movement

Unlike the Roman Catholic Church, the Orthodox Church has taken an active part in the ecumenical movement that was publicly inaugurated at the Universal Christian Conference on Life and Work held in Stockholm in 1925 and which led, at the conference in Amsterdam in 1948, to the formation of the World Council of Churches. A large number of Orthodox churches are members of the World Council of Churches; Orthodox ecclesiastics and theologians serve on its committees and attend its conferences.

1. RELATIONSHIP TO THE REFORMED CHURCHES

In the Sixteenth and Seventeenth Centuries

There is a long history behind the Orthodox Church's collaboration with the ecumenical movement and the World Council of Churches. Indeed, it goes back to the time of the Reformation when direct relations were established between German Protestant theologians and the Patriarch of Constantinople. The first overtures were made by Philipp Melanchthon, who communicated with the Patriarch of Constantinople through a former secretary of the patriarchate who called on him in Wittenberg. Melanchthon profited by the occasion to work out a Greek translation of the Augsburg Confession. The translation, however, was not sent to Constantinople until the end of the sixteenth century, when Protestant envoys dispatched by the theological faculty of Tübingen University handed it to Patriarch Jeremias II. The patriarch's reply marked the first phase of a new era of theological thinking within the Orthodox Church. Although Orthodoxy had little understanding of the tenets of the Reformers her theologians could not refrain from plunging into the struggle being waged in the West over the definition of the "pure doctrine." Orthodoxy embarked upon a phase that present-day Orthodox theologians have justly called "pseudomorphosis" in which Orthodoxy felt herself obliged to take positions on problems alien to her. In these controversies the Orthodox theologians frequently adopted the terminology of the contending parties of the West.

Symptomatic of Orthodoxy's shifting sympathies was the procession of pro-Rome and pro-Reform patriarchs of Byzantium. Often they would hold their patriarchal throne a few months only to be overthrown by conspiracies within their own ranks or by intrigues conducted among the rival European powers at the Sublime Porte. The most important personality of this turbulent era in the history of the Greek Church was Patriarch Cyril Lukaris. His *Confession of Faith*, published in Geneva, brought Orthodox doctrine extremely close to Protestantism. He fell victim, however, to the combined intrigues of the Jesuits, the Catholic powers and enemies in his own Orthodox camp and in 1638 was executed on the order of the sultan in Constantinople. A fine specimen of "pseudomorphosis" was the polemic writ-

ten against his *Confession* by Peter Mogila, wherein Roman
Catholic arguments are mustered to attack Patriarch
Cyril's Reformed creed.

The Era of Peter the Great

The Orthodox dislike for Rome, which grew stronger
after the Union of Brest (1596) had established a united
Catholic Church under Polish auspices, impelled numerous
young Orthodox theologians to attend Protestant univer-
sities in Germany, Switzerland and England, since there
were no Orthodox academies in the Orthodox countries
under Turkish rule. In this way not only Reformed ideas
but Protestant educational methods found their way into
Orthodoxy. Both the Russian and the Greek Orthodox
churches approached particularly close to German Protestantism during the heyday of Pietism. This tendency was
fostered by Peter the Great, who had great sympathy for
what he regarded as the more progressive character of
European Protestantism. Peter undertook to reform the
constitution of the Orthodox Church, abolished the old
patriarchate, and patterned his new synodal constitution
on the organization of the German Protestant territorial
churches. Russian translations of German religious writings,
such as Johann Arndt's *Four Books of True Christianity,*
commissioned and printed in Halle by August Hermann
Francke, were widely disseminated among the Orthodox.

The Holy Alliance

The era of the Holy Alliance, the pact of 1815 wherein
Orthodox Russia, Catholic Austria and Protestant Prussia,
having waged a joint struggle against Napoleon, now committed themselves to a continuing friendship, encouraged a
new and more intensive rapprochement and collaboration between Russian Orthodoxy and German Protestantism. It laid the groundwork for the chief ecumenical ideas
that a century later were to be realized in practice. Franz
von Baader, himself a Roman Catholic, summed up the

new attitude in a formula that was echoed by many Protestants: *Audiatur et tertia pars!*—The third party must also be heard! At the heart of this formula was the recognition that the Reformation was a specifically Western reaction to a specifically Occidental form of Christianity, namely Roman Catholicism, but that the Roman Catholic Church and the Protestant churches by no means represented the whole of Christendom. Rather, the schism that resulted from the Reformation was to be understood as a product of the far older schism between Rome and Byzantium, which had resulted from the West's embracing of the idea of Roman primacy in the ninth century. A genuine ecumenical meeting of minds, therefore, could take place only if the Orthodox Church were included. The modern ecumenical movement rests upon awareness of this essential point.

2. RELATIONSHIP TO THE ANGLICAN CHURCH

Orthodoxy's relations with the independent Protestant churches of England and North America have been darkened by the fact that these churches conducted missions in the territory of the Orthodox national churches of Greece, the Near East and Egypt and tried to make converts even among the Orthodox. Nevertheless, there were early Orthodox efforts toward rapprochement with the Anglican Church, and in some cases these led to shared communion. The roots of this amity go back to the eighteenth century. Fresh efforts were made in the thirties and forties of the nineteenth century, as a result of the emergence of the High Church movement in Oxford, which stressed acceptance of episcopal organization and apostolic succession as the dogmatic basis of catholicity. Ever since, discussion has centered primarily upon the question of the Eastern Orthodox Church's recognition of Anglican ordinations. In the course of this debate the two churches moved closer together or farther apart according to the vagaries of national and ecclesiastical policy within the complicated structure of the British Empire. However much the two churches might disagree on dogma, a cordial feeling prevailed. For one thing, the Anglican Church did not attempt to proselytize among Orthodox believers when these came within its scope, as they so often did, England being the occupying power not only in the Near East but also in India. Hence Anglicans were constantly thrown into contact with members of Orthodox national churches in large portions of the world, and on the whole got on well with them.

In 1841 an Anglo-Prussian episcopate was established in Jerusalem, with its bishop ordained according to the Anglican rite. This Jerusalem diocese included all the Protestants of the Holy Land. When it was set up, it explicitly acknowledged the traditional rights of the old Orthodox episcopates and patriarchates and pledged itself to refrain from missionary activity among Orthodox Christians.

3. WHY ORTHODOXY HAS COLLABORATED WITH THE ECUMENICAL MOVEMENT

External and Internal Reasons

Many cultural, social and political motives have been advanced as reasons for Orthodoxy's participation in the ecumenical movement—a participation which, incidentally, many within the Church strongly oppose. It has been pointed out that the Orthodox Church, compelled to be permanently on guard against Rome because of the continual machinations of the Roman Catholic Church and its attempted incursions into the ranks of the Orthodox, has necessarily turned for help to the non-Roman churches. The Orthodox youth in particular, it has been said, have felt the attraction of the progressive cultural, social and civilizatory spirit of the Protestant churches and have favored collaboration with them.

But apart from all such external reasons, it is clear that

a spontaneous ecumenical tendency exists within the Orthodox Church. The Church in fact calls itself "the ecumenical
Church." In so titling itself the Eastern Church is appealing
directly to those Christians who do not belong to the Orthodox Church, being separated from it by schism or heresy.
No other Church has prayed so fervently and naturally,
throughout its entire history, for unity of the Church. To
this day the Orthodox Church liturgy regularly includes
the prayer of Ephraem the Syrian (c. 306–73): "Lord
God who settest the erring on the right path, who reunitest
the dispersed and preservest the unity of those who are now
together, we pray Thee, gather Thy Church in unity of
faith, that we may serve one another in obedience to Thy
truth and may confess and praise Thee with one mouth,
through our Lord Jesus Christ, Thy Son, who lives with
Thee and the Holy Ghost and reigns from eternity to
eternity. Amen!"

It is significant that the Orthodox Church put forth the
most vigorous practical ecumenical proposals even before
the Conference on Life and Work at Stockholm in 1925.
In 1920 the acting Ecumenical Patriarch, reacting to the
terrible persecutions of the Church in the Soviet Union, sent
a circular letter signed by eleven other Orthodox metropolitans to all "Churches of Christ wherever they may be,"
calling for the establishment of a league of churches corresponding to the League of Nations. Such a league, he said,
would abet the restitution of spiritual dignity to the whole
of humanity against the internal and external dangers of
global materialism.

If we keep in mind that this same Orthodox Church
holds unshakably to the conviction that it alone is the
catholic apostolic Church of Jesus Christ, we may find it
hard to reconcile this exclusive dogmatic position with the
Church's ecumenical liberality in practice. This attitude
becomes more logical when we remember that Orthodoxy
insists upon the primacy of love rather than the primacy
of justice (see p. 51 ff.). The Orthodox Church's partici-

pation in the ecumenical movement is a typical Orthodox inconsistency. Her position is this: Even though the Orthodox Church is the only Church of Jesus Christ, membership in this Church imposes upon its members an attitude of love toward other Christian churches. The Orthodox Church, because of its own ecumenical nature, can adopt an unprejudiced stand toward non-Orthodox Christians and churches without abandoning its own claim. Thus it participates without condescension and without fears in the work of the World Council of Churches.

Opposition

We cannot, however, ignore the countercurrents within the Orthodox Church and the arguments that opponents have raised to the Church's involving herself with the World Council of Churches. Political factors play a large part in this opposition. Such factors, for example, were clearly present in the decision of the Moscow Synod of 1948, whose sharp repudiation of the ecumenical movement and rejection of the overtures of the Anglican Church was entirely in the spirit of the then current Stalinist foreign policy, whose slogans were, revealingly enough, repeated. There are also the serious objections raised by those who point out that in entering the ecumenical movement the Orthodox Church is instituting amicable relations with the very churches that have hitherto regarded the Orthodox lands as a missionary field and have sometimes behaved quite ruthlessly in this respect. Even where the pressure of proselytism has abated or where it has been deliberately eschewed, such modern Christian world youth organizations as the YMCA, YWCA and the World Student Christian Federation (WSCF), whose attitudes are fundamentally ecumenical, are suspected of secret Protestant missionary aims. Many conservative members of the Orthodox Church regard these organizations as Trojan horses that have been brought within the walls of Orthodoxy in the name of the Universal Church, but which in reality contain armed bands of Protestant missionaries. Moreover, these ecumenical organizations, which exert a strong attraction upon the Orthodox youth of the Near East and Egypt, are fundamentally liberal in theology. To the eyes of many Orthodox conservatives they are a form of Freemasonry in Christian camouflage. Conservative Orthodox circles often express the same doubts about the World Council of Churches, which includes many denominations whose dogmas are miles apart from the tenets of the Orthodox faith. Moreover, many members of the churches of Asia Minor, Egypt and Ethiopia regard the non-Orthodox forms of Christianity primarily as the religions of their former occupation powers or colonial masters, to whose dominion they were exposed for centuries. When new YMCA centers are built in Orthodox cities of the Near East, the people tend to look upon the matter as merely another offshoot of drilling for oil, on a par with the establishment of new refineries, pipelines and airports.

In the field of dogma, too, there are theologians who would prefer a strictly exclusive attitude toward Orthodox doctrines. They feel that the Orthodox cause is being betrayed if Orthodox theologians as much as engage in a discussion about the principles of the faith with the non-Orthodox. Even those theologians who are ready to participate in ecumenical work sometimes complain that the theological aspect of Orthodoxy is not taken seriously enough within the ecumenical movement, even when all due respect is shown to the Orthodox members.

Consequences of Collaboration

All these objections, however, have as yet not seriously upset the fundamentally affirmative attitude of Orthodoxy toward the ecumenical movement. The collaboration has proved to be useful to both sides and a valuable enrichment to both. The Protestant churches find it wonderfully rewarding to join in theological efforts with churches that have preserved the doctrinal and liturgical traditions of the primitive Church through centuries of the severest persecution and tribulation. Such churches have retained a continuity of views and types of worship that churches of the modern Western type might easily come to dismiss as outmoded. A closer knowledge of the character of the Eastern Church, however, corrects this tendency. On the other hand, it is of the greatest importance to the Orthodox Church, whose intellectual development has been handicapped by centuries of repression under non-Christian and deliberately anti-Christian forces, to engage in a vital confrontation with types of Christian ecclesiasticism that have attempted, under more favorable conditions, to assimilate all the political, social, technological and cultural trends of modern times and to find new forms of religious expression, community living and education. The future of the ecumenical movement promises to provide fruitful stimulus and enrichment to both sides.

XIV.

Greatness and Weakness of Orthodoxy

1. THE STRENGTH OF ORTHODOXY

Within contemporary Christendom, Orthodoxy shines with a light all its own. Especially impressive is the fact that it has preserved faithfully the catholicity of the primitive Church. This is true for all its vital functions.

Its liturgy is a wonderful repository of all the early Church's interpretations and practices of worship. Whatever the early Church and the Byzantine Church created in the way of liturgical drama, meditation and contemplation, in beauty of prayers and hymns, has been integrated and retained in the Orthodox liturgy. Similarly the content of Scripture has been kept ever present in the form of generous readings from both the Old and the New Testaments at various prescribed times through the liturgical year. The entire historical tradition of the Church is constantly communicated to the members in readings from the lives of the great saints and mystics (see p. 27 ff.). The sermon has its fixed place in the sacramental service; originally it came immediately after the reading of the Gospel text in the service for catechumens, but nowadays it frequently comes elsewhere—for example, after Communion. Verbal service and sacramental service are meaningfully interlocked so that total separation of them, such as has occurred in Western Reformed churches, can never occur. The full doctrine of the early Church, as it was defined by the seven ecumenical councils, is immediate and vital in the liturgy, and also in the hymn of worship that elaborates the fundamental ideas of both Orthodox and lay prayer. Here there is no divorce between liturgy and theology, worship and dogma.

This Church has clung to the original consciousness of universality and catholicity. Its sense of itself as the one holy, ecumenical and apostolic Church is based not upon a judicial idea, but upon the consciousness of representing the Mystical Body of Christ. According to the Orthodox outlook, the celestial and the earthly Church, and the Church of the dead, belong indissolubly together. In taking part in the liturgy the earthly Church is reminded that it belongs to the higher Church. In the liturgy the earthly congregation experiences the presence of the angels, patriarchs, prophets, apostles, martyrs, saints and all the redeemed; in the sacrament of the Eucharist it experiences the Presence of its Lord. Within the Mystical Body there takes place a unique communication and correlation: within that communion the gifts of the Holy Spirit—the power to forgive sins, to transmit salvation, to suffer by proxy for one another, and the power of intercession—become effective. And these powers extend down to the domain of the dead, for God is "a Lord of the living, not the dead."

In this way the Church has preserved the early Christian combination of genuine personalism, of appreciation for the uniqueness and singularity of the individual, along with the early Christian sense of communion. But the catholicity of the Orthodox Church is not in any way synonymous with uniformity. Thanks to its principle of letting every people possess the gospel, liturgy and doctrine in its own language,

Orthodoxy has been able to adapt to the natural national differences within mankind. The broad framework of Orthodoxy has been able to accommodate a wealth of ecclesiastical traditions. The result has been that the Orthodox Church has shown itself as an extraordinarily creative force. It has exerted great religious, social and ethical influence upon the cultures of Orthodox nations and taken a leading part in the intellectual and political development of those nations. This function of the Orthodox Church has been especially significant during the periods in which the political existence of Orthodox nations was threatened or destroyed.

Orthodoxy's unity within variety has been sustained by a unified canon of the New and Old Testaments, by a unified episcopal organization based on apostolic succession, by a unified liturgy that is the same in all languages, and by unity of doctrine and dogmatic tradition.

The durability of the Orthodox Church is all the more remarkable in that it has been exposed to enormous historical disasters, to persecutions of all kinds, especially from Islam; in great stretches of its former dominions, Orthodoxy has been completely exterminated. Nevertheless it has adhered with the greatest loyalty, down to the present day, to the early Church's liturgical and dogmatic heritage.

This heritage is not at all a museum piece as has often been asserted. On the contrary, it is a living force capable of development. In a certain sense the greatness of Orthodoxy rests on the very fact that the doctrine is not so carefully defined down to details, is not so strictly regulated by canons. Orthodoxy's system is by no means closed; it is still full of potential. The charismatic life of Orthodoxy has not been confined within sets of legal and institutional forms. There is a significant degree of intellectual mobility, even in theology; thus, teachers of theology are frequently laymen rather than ordained priests. Alongside the offices of deacon, priest and bishop, the Church has from the beginning left room for the charismatic office of the teacher—*didaskalos.*

A further essential trait of the Orthodox Church is Christian universalism. This manifests itself in Orthodoxy's view of the cosmos as well as its view of history. Western Christianity has more or less underplayed the question of a Christian natural philosophy. The Eastern Church, on the other hand, has endeavored to frame its Christian interpretation of creation in an unending series of sketches for a Christian cosmology and natural philosophy. It views the process of redemption not only as an event that has taken place for the benefit of man, within the framework of human history, but also as a cosmic event in which the evolution of the entire universe is included. Anthropology, cosmology and the doctrine of salvation are indissolubly interconnected. According to the Orthodox theory, the fall of man carried along the entire universe into rebellion against God, exposing everything to the powers of sin and death. Similarly, the incarnation of God in Jesus Christ and his resurrection likewise had cosmic effects. The "whole of creation" participated in the salvation brought by Christ, and all creatures yearn for the day of redemption along with man. Thus, at the end of time, when salvation is fulfilled, the old earth and the old heaven will be transformed along with man into a new earth and a new heaven. The reshaping of creation will involve the entire universe.

This universalism is also magnificently present in the Church's interpretation of redemption. It does not restrict the effects of divine redemption to the narrow confines traditionally promised by the Old Testament. According to the Orthodox Church, it is not only the Chosen People, but all the peoples of the globe who are involved in the story of man's redemption. The universalism of Orthodox thought is based upon the doctrine of the Logos. Orthodox theologians grant that the divine Logos spoke chiefly through the voices of the Old Testament prophets before the Incarnation, but there are evidences of his presence among other peoples. Both Clement of Alexandria and Origen pointed out that traces of the divine Logos could also be found in Greek, Indian, Egyptian and Persian philosophy. Thus all of mankind has been from the beginning included in the history of redemption, a history whose culmination and fulfillment is to be found in Jesus Christ.

Another element making for the greatness of Orthodoxy is its unwavering emphasis on the idea of God's beauty. Its prayers and hymns have never ceased to praise the beauty of God. This picture of God does not accord with the picture of a wrathful God of justice and predestination as has been painted by Occidental theology. It can only be tenable if paired with a universalism that sees Christ as the perfector of the cosmos and of salvation, as the conqueror not only of sin but also of physical annihilation, as the victor over death and the demonic powers of the entire cosmos.

In consequence, Orthodoxy has preserved the original mood of the Christian fellowships, the *chara*—rejoicing and jubilation—which the New Testament mentions as the characteristic spirit of the first Christian fellowship. This rejoicing has remained the fundamental mood of divine service in the Orthodox Church, especially of the Eucharistic service: joy in union with the living Lord; jubilation that the powers of sin and death have been overcome, the demons defeated, and that the reign of Satan has already been shattered. Its basic assumption is that at bottom evil is already overcome, that to the reborn the new eon of life in God, of glory in God and the beauty of God, the life of new creatures in a new cosmos, has already dawned.

2. THE WEAKNESSES OF ORTHODOXY

The validity of the Orthodox Church has always depended on its maintaining an equilibrium among the various vital spheres on which it touches. Whenever that equilibrium has been upset, the Orthodox Church has, historically, been exposed to four dangers.

Establishment

The first danger is inherent in the nature of the Church as an "established" church. Because of this, any displacement of the equilibrium between state and Church in favor of the state will have unfortunate results. True, Orthodox doctrine upholds the ideal of "harmony" or "symphony" between state and Church. But in the history of Orthodoxy the balance has shifted, time and time again, to the point at which the state outweighs the Church. In Orthodox countries the Church is constantly in danger of losing its internal freedom to the state. This has indeed happened repeatedly, especially in Russia. Even today the tradition of the Russian established Church continues to operate. Although the Russian Church today lives in an atheistic state, whose constitution proclaims the complete separation of Church and state, the old tradition of the establishment comes to the fore again and again, and the hierarchy permits itself to be used as an instrument of the Soviet Union's internal and foreign policy.

On the whole Orthodoxy's relation to the state has had unfortunate consequences; the Church has suffered from the union. The state has been led to influence excessively the inner life and organization of the Church, employing for this purpose methods inappropriate to the nature of the Church. It has adapted Christianity to the aims and advantages of the state. The Church has been seduced into using the political and police powers of the state when it should have employed the means peculiar to its own nature as a spiritual institution. All this gave rise to the suspicion, which having once struck root was hard to dislodge, that the Church's basic aim was something other than giving man, through the gospel, faith and the freedom of the children of God. The most pernicious effect, however, was this: the existence of an established Church made the gospel a law for those who did not believe in it. This was alienating Christianity from its true nature, which is to be a law only for those who are reborn in God.

Nationalism (Phyletism)

The second danger lay in a displacement of the equilibrium between the ecumenical and the nationalistic spirit of the Orthodox Church in favor of nationalism. This danger of nationalism was already implicit in the peculiar structure of Orthodoxy which permitted each nation its own language, constitution and ecclesiastical autonomy. Thus the development of the Church was intimately connected with the development of state and nation in the history of Russia, and above all in the history of the Balkan peoples.

We have already seen that the attempt by the Bulgarian Church to free itself from the ecumenical patriarchate of Constantinople and to set up its own autocephalous national church, was branded as a heresy—"phyletism"—by the Greek patriarch. In point of fact phyletism is a latent heresy that has constantly threatened the entire Orthodox world. Modern Orthodox efforts to achieve closer ties among the member churches have only revealed that national egoism is stronger than the consciousness of membership in a universal church. Even among the emigrant churches with their ecumenically minded world organizations, such as Syndesmos, a league of Orthodox youth organizations, national tensions are forever asserting themselves. Grave difficulties crop up in any collaboration among Greeks, Arabs and Slavs. And in Syria, Palestine and Egypt, joint work between the Greek and Arab or Coptic portions of the Church has been impeded by rivalries for spiritual and practical leadership within the Church. Too frequently Orthodoxy failed to prove itself a bond of spiritual unity sufficiently strong to overcome the nationalistic quarrels among the Balkan peoples. The Orthodox Church has never been able to prevent these conflicts from precipitating terrible carnage. The emigrant churches, too, are rent by nationalistic disputes. To the outsider they present a painful picture of nationalistic and political dissensions that make a mockery of the ecumenical claims of Orthodoxy.

Independence in the Liturgy

The third peril lies in a displacement of the equilibrium between sacrament and social work accompanied by propagation of the faith, in favor of sacrament. This might be termed the danger of liturgical isolationism. When the liturgical and sacramental elements become preponderant, the liturgy can easily become a shell into which the Church withdraws like a turtle, losing all contact with living reality. This danger of liturgical isolationism is inherent in the very nature of Orthodoxy. Political conditions, however, have intensified this tendency. The holders of political power have always been only too pleased when the Church confined itself to its liturgical, sacramental functions and withdrew from its other obligation, such as propagating the faith by active preaching, or seeking the realization of Christian ethics within the body politic. The Orthodox tsars, emperors and kings, as well as their present atheistic successors, have as a rule encouraged the liturgical self-isolation of the Church. In this way they hoped to render the Church innocuous and to divert it from its further purpose of shaping the world along Christian lines.

This bent has been furthered by the fact that most Orthodox churches were for centuries forced to lead at best a tolerated life under rulers and governments of alien faiths. Under the dominion of Mongols, Arabs and Turks the various Orthodox churches of Russia and the Near and Middle East, have in fact crawled back into their liturgical shell and have necessarily renounced outward activity. It is therefore not surprising that the Orthodox Church in Russia today, with its history of centuries of such self-isolation under non-Christian governments, under Bolshevism has once again taken refuge in an attitude of liturgical isolationism. This position has one great virtue: it protects Orthodoxy in a remarkable manner against the intrusion of non-Christian influences into its innermost realm of liturgy. But on the other hand this long-standing attitude of self-isolation can easily become a condition of permanent paralysis.

Renunciation of the "World"

In saying this we have already forecast the fourth danger: the displacement of equilibrium between transcendentalism and Christianity's task of renewing the world, in favor of transcendentalism. In divine worship the Orthodox Christian experiences an encounter with the celestial Church, with the kingdom of heaven. Out of this encounter grace, forgiveness, hope and salvation pour down upon him. Under the pressure of political events the Orthodox believer manifests a tendency to excessive otherworldliness that keeps him from engaging in the Christian's specific task of being a "co-worker of God" who, as the Apostle Paul says, will shape the world in the spirit of Christ. Here again the tendency to renounce both social activity and the cultural fulfillment of the Church is reinforced. Significantly enough, the kind of Christian mysticism Eastern Orthodoxy has produced tends to make the world and even fellowmen vanish from the gaze of the believer. There is no neighbor left to love; there remains only the inner meeting between the self and the transcendental, in which ultimately even the self is submerged and disappears. Thus Orthodoxy has often all too readily excused itself from the task of shaping the world in a Christian sense and has consoled itself with the thought that in any case this world will remain "of evil" until Judgment Day. Most of the social movements in Russian politics have come not from Orthodox believers, but from opponents of the Church and religion—in contrast to the Anglo-Saxon countries, where conscious Christians—especially those belonging to free

churches—have for the most part been in the forefront of
all the movements for social betterment.

3. CAN THESE WEAKNESSES BE OVERCOME?

These weaknesses, however, can be overcome. Orthodoxy contains within itself the spiritual strength to correct
these disequilibriums. But that is not entirely a matter of
free choice. The restoration of the equilibrium between
state and Church in most cases—and certainly in the Soviet
Union—depends almost exclusively upon the attitude of the
state, that is, upon its readiness to permit the Church a
fair degree of activity in public life. The history of Orthodoxy shows that a responsible leadership of the Church
can go far in reinvigorating the social dynamism of the
Church even after long paralysis—provided such a leadership keeps the end in view, namely, a Christian reshaping
of the world.

The evils of nationalism can likewise be overcome. Here,
too, the history of the Orthodox Church shows that the
ecumenical idea can form the basis for genuine collaboration among national churches extremely different in habits
and languages. The modern ecumenical movement whose
outlines we have traced has certainly brought about a re-
awakening of the feeling of identity among various national Orthodox churches. It has brought about a return of
the original ecumenical consciousness of Orthodoxy, a re-
discovery of Orthodoxy's "internal universalism."

The danger of liturgical isolationism, too, can be conquered. The liturgy does not necessarily have to drive the
Church into self-isolation. On the contrary, it can serve the
Church as the source of a fresh access of spirit and vitality. The liturgy contains within itself forces that could
revive the theology and the mysticism of the Church and
could lead to the sanctification and Christian shaping of all
of life. It can also spur a revival of preaching. For it is
significant that wherever in the world violent repression has

receded and Orthodox revival movements have arisen, these movements have taken their inspiration from the liturgy and have looked to it for the source of their vitality.

We all know the biblical story of Moses in the wilderness and how he saw a bush that "was burning, yet it was not consumed" (Ex. 3:2). And "the angel of the Lord appeared to him in a flame of fire out of the midst of a bush." When he went up to it "God called to him out of the bush. . . . 'Do not come near; put off your shoes from your feet, for the place on which you are standing is holy ground.' "

Orthodoxy has incorporated into its liturgy the various typological interpretations that the great ascetics have given to this scene. Orthodoxy sees in it three mysteries:

The mystery of the Holy Trinity:

"As Thou hast appeared to Moses in the thornbush in the form of fire, Thou wast called angel, Word of the Father, who revealedst Thy coming to us, whereby Thou plainly proclaimedst to all men the tripersonal power of the one Deity."

The mystery of the Incarnation:

"As the Mysteries tell us, Moses foresaw in holy vision Thine image: the thornbush not burning in the fire, O Virgin, O sublime one beyond all reproach. For the Maker, dwelling in Thee, did not burn Thee who art elevated above all things made, Bride of God."

The mystery of the Mother of God:

"Thou wert imaged long ago by the thornbush on Sinai, which did not burn, O Virgin, in the touch of the fire. For as a Virgin thou didst bear. And exceeding all sense thou, Mother-Virgin, hast remained Virgin."

But in the deepest sense the Orthodox Church itself—sprung from the mystery of the Incarnation and preserving that mystery in itself, sprouting in the wilderness as the Church of ascetics, ravaged by the sandstorms of persecution, harassed by enemies of the faith and hostile fellows of the same faith, parched by immeasurable suffering and by inner and outer temptations, but yet unconsumed; burning with the fire of the Holy Spirit, aglow with the love of God, irradiated by the nuptial joy of the heavenly feast, illumined by the all-transfiguring power of the resurrected Lord—the Orthodox Church itself is

THE BURNING BUSH.

Bibliography[1]

General Works, Surveys, Introductions

ADENEY, W. F.: *The Greek and Eastern Churches.* New York, 1928.

AMMANN, A. M.: *Ostslawische Kirchengeschichte.* Vienna, 1950.

ARSENIEW, N. V.: *Die Kirche des Morgenlandes. Weltanschauung und Frömmigkeitsleben.* (Sammlung Göschen) Berlin-Leipzig: Walter de Gruyter, 1926.

———: *Von dem Geist und dem Glauben der Kirche des Ostens.* Leipzig, 1941.

ATTWATER, D.: *The Christian Churches of the East.* Vol. I: *Churches in Communion with Rome,* Milwaukee, 1948. Vol. II: *Churches not in Communion with Rome,* Milwaukee, 1947–48.

BENZ, E.: "Die russische Kirche und das abendländische Christentum." In: *Zeitschrift für Religions- und Geistes-*

---

[1] Contains only references in German, French and English. References in Russian, New Greek and other foreign languages are omitted.

geschichte, ed. by H. J. Schoeps, Marburg, 1. Jg., Heft 1, 1948.

——: *Russische Kirche und östl. Christentum.* (Mit Beiträgen von Hildegard Schaeder, E. Benz, L. Müller, R. Schneider, ed. by E. Benz) Tübingen, 1949.

——: *Die abendländische Sendung der östlich-orthodoxen Kirche. Akademie d. Wissenschaften u. d. Literatur in Mainz. Abh. d. Geistes- u. sozialwiss. Klasse,* Jg. 1950, Nr. 8.

BETH, K.: *Die orientalische Christenheit der Mittelmeerländer. Reisestudien zur Statistik und Symbolik.* Berlin, 1902.

BONWETSCH, N.: "Griechisch-orthodoxes Christentum und Kirche." In: *Die Kultur der Gegenwart,* 1/4, 2d ed., 1909.

BUBNOFF-EHRENBERG: *Östliches Christentum, Dokumente,* ed. by N. v. Bubnoff and H. Ehrenberg. Vol. II: *Philosophie.* Munich, 1925.

FRIZ, K.: *Die Stimme der Ostkirche.* Stuttgart, 1950.

HEILER, F.: *Urkirche und Ostkirche* (*Die katholische Kirche des Ostens und Westens,* Vol. I). Munich, 1937.

MULERT, H.: *Christentum und Kirche in Russland und dem Orient.* In: *Religionsgeschichtl. Volksbücher f. d. deutsche christl. Gegenwart,* IV. Reihe, 22/23. Heft. Tübingen: J.C.B. Mohr, 1916.

SERAPHIM (Metropolitan): *Die Ostkirche.* 1st ed. Stuttgart, 1950.

STANLEY, A. P.: *Lectures on the History of the Eastern Church.* London, 1924.

DE VRIES, SJ, W.: *Der christliche Osten in Geschichte und Gegenwart.* In: *Das östliche Christentum.* Abh., N. F., Heft 12. Würzburg, 1951.

WUNDERLE, G.: *Das geistige Antlitz der Ostkirche.* Augustinus Verlag, Würzburg, 1949.

ZANKOV, st.: *Die orthodoxe Kirche des Ostens in ökumenischer Sicht.* Zürich, 1946.

For Chapter I: The Orthodox Icon

AINALOW, D.: *Geschichte der russischen Monumentalkunst der vormoskowitischen Zeit.* Berlin-Leipzig, 1932.

——: *Geschichte der russischen Monumentalkunst der vormongolischen Zeit.* Berlin-Leipzig, 1932.

ALPATOW, M., and N. BRUNOW: *Geschichte der altrussischen Kunst.* Augsburg, 1932.

BALTRUSAITIS, J.: *Etudes sur l'art médiéval en Géorgie et en Arménie.* Paris, 1929.

FILOW, B.: *Geschichte der altbulgarischen Kunst.* Berlin-Leipzig, 1932.

ONASCH, K.: *König des Alls. Bildmeditationen über das Leben Christi.* Berlin, 1952.

ROTHEMUND, H. J.: *Ikonenkunst. Ein Handbuch.* Munich, 1954.

SCHWEINFURTH, PH.: *Geschichte der russischen Malerei im Mittelalter.* The Hague, 1930.

——: *Grundzüge der Byzantinisch-Osteuropäischen Kunstgeschichte.* Berlin, 1947.

USPENSKIJ-LOSSKIJ: *Der Sinn der Ikonen.* Bern and Olten, 1952.

WENDT, C. H.: *Rumänische Ikonenmalerei.* Eisenach, 1953.

For Chapter II: Liturgy and Sacraments

ALIVISATOS, H. S.: "Der Kultus der Kirche." In: *Ekklesia,* Vol. X, Leipzig, 1939.

BACHMANN, EVA-MARIA: *Der Gottesdienst der russisch-orthodoxen Kirche.* Berlin, 1954.

BEHR-SIGEL, E.: *Prière et Sainteté dans l'église Russe.* Paris, 1950.

BRIGHTMAN, F. E., ed.: *Liturgies, Eastern and Western, being the Texts Original or Translated of the Principal Liturgies of the Church.* Vol. 1: *Eastern Liturgies.* Oxford, 1896.

KIRCHHOFF, K.: *Über dich freut sich der Erdkreis. Marien-hymnen der byzantinischen Kirche*. Münster i. W., 1940.
——: *Ehre sei Gott. Dreifaltigkeitshymnen d. byzant. Kirche*. Münster, 1940.
——: *In Paradisum. Totenhymnen d. byzant. Kirche*. Münster, 1940.
——: *Osterjubel der Ostkirche*, I and II. Münster, n.d.
MATZERATH, O.: *Busse und hl. Ölung in der byzantinischen Kirche. Heilige Feiern der Ostkirche III*. Ed. by Monks of the Abbey of St. Joseph in Gerleve. Paderborn, n.d.
——: *Die Totenfeiern der byzantinischen Kirche. Heilige Feiern der Ostkirche II*. Paderborn, n.d.
ROSE, K.: *Predigt der russisch-orthodoxen Kirche*. Berlin, 1952.
TYCIAK, J.: *Die Liturgie als Quelle östlicher Frömmigkeit*. In: *Ecclesia Orans. Zur Einführung in den Geist der Liturgie*, Vol. XX, Freiburg im Breisgau, 1937.

For Chapter III: Dogma

ARSENIEW, N. V.: *Die Kirche des Morgenlandes, Weltanschauung und Frömmigkeitsleben*. Berlin, 1926.
BULGAKOV, S.: *The Orthodox Church*. London?, 1935.
FORTESCUE, A.: *The Orthodox Eastern Church*. London, 1929.
HEILER, Fr.: *Urkirche und Ostkirche (Die katholische Kirche des Ostens und Westens*, Vol. I). Munich, 1937.
JANIN, R.: *Les Églises orientales et les Rites orientaux*. 3d ed. Paris, 1935.
——: *Les Églises séparées d'Orient*. Paris, 1929. Tr. by P. Boylan as *The Separated Eastern Churches*. St. Louis, Mo., 1933.
KIDD, B. J.: *The Churches of Eastern Christendom from A.D. 451 to the Present Time*. London, 1927.
MICHALCESCU, J.: *Die Bekenntnisse und die wichtigsten Glaubenszeugnisse der griechisch-orientalischen Kirche*

im Original text nebst einleitenden Bemerkungen. Intro. by D. A. Hauck. Leipzig, 1904.

TYCIAK, J.: *Wege östlicher Theologie.* Bonn, 1946.

ZANDER, L.: "Die Weisheit Gottes im russischen Glauben und Denken." In: *Kerygma und Dogma,* Jg. 2, Heft 1, 1956.

ZANKOV, ST.: *Das orthodoxe Christentum des Ostens, sein Wesen und seine gegenwärtige Gestalt.* Berlin, 1928. Tr. and ed. by Donald A. Lowrie as *The Eastern Orthodox Church.* London, 1929.

For Chapter IV: Constitution and Law
of the Orthodox Church

ALIVISATOS, H. S.: "Das kanonische Recht der orthodoxen Kirche." In: *Ekklesia,* Vol. X, Leipzig, 1939.

MILASCH, N.: *Das Kirchenrecht der morgenländischen Kirche,* Mostar 2, 1905.

SILBERNAGL, J.: *Verfassung und gegenwärtiger Bestand sämtlicher Kirchen des Orients.* 2d ed. Regensburg, 1904.

For Chapter V: National Churches,
Schismatic Churches, Emigrant Churches

ALEXEEV, W.: *Russian Orthodox Bishops in the Soviet Union, 1941–1953. Materials for the History of the Russian Orthodox Church in the USSR.* New York, 1954.

ANDERSON, P. B.: *People, Church and State in Modern Russia.* London, 1944.

BONWETSCH, N.: *Kirchengeschichte Russlands im Abriss.* Leipzig, 1923.

BRIEM, E.: *Kommunismus und Religion in der Sowjetunion. Ein Ideenkampf.* Tr. from the Swedish by E. Schaper. Basel, n.d.

CURTISS, J. SH.: *The Russian Church and the Soviet State, 1917–1950.* Boston, 1953.

KOVALEVSKY, P.: *La dispersion Russe à travers le monde et son rôle culturel.* Chauny (Aisne), 1951.

ROSE, K.: *Drei Patriarchen von Moskau und ganz Russland.* Berlin, 1952.

SPULER, B.: "Die russische orthodoxe Kirche 1951." In: *Osteuropa,* February 1952.

——: "Die Gegenwartslage der Ostkirchen in ihrer völkischen und staatlichen Umwelt." In: *Bücher des Wissens,* Vol. 6, Wiesbaden, 1948.

For Chapter VI: Monasticism

ARSENIEW, N. V.: *Ostkirche und Mystik.* 2d ed. Munich, 1943.

BUBNOFF, N. V.: *Russische Frömmigkeit. Briefe eines Starzen.* Wiesbaden, 1947.

FALLMERAYER, J. Ph.: *Der heilige Berg Athos.* Dortmund, 1947.

GOETZ, L. K.: *Das Kiewer Höhlenkloster als Kulturzentrum des vormongolischen Russland.* Passau, 1904.

Kallistus und Ignatius: Das Herzensgebet Mystik und Yoga der Ostkirche. Die Centurie der Mönche Kallistus und Ignatius. In: *Dokumente religiöser Erfahrung,* ed. by A. Rosenberg. Munich-Planegg: O. W. Barth, 1955.

KOLOGRIWOF, I. V.: *Von Hellas zum Mönchtum. Leben und Denken Konstantin Leontjews (1831–1891).* Regensburg, 1948.

LOSSKY, Vl: *Essai sur la Théologie Mystique de l'Église d'Orient.* Paris, 1944. Tr. as *The Mystical Theology of the Eastern Church.* London, 1957.

ROUËT DE JOURNEL, M.-J.: *Monachisme et Monastères Russes.* Paris: Payot, 1952.

SIMEON THE THEOLOGIAN: *Licht vom Licht, Hymnen.* German trans. by K. Kirchhoff. Munich, 1951.

SMOLITSCH, I.: *Leben und Lehre der Starzen.* 2d ed. Köln-Olten, 1952.

——: *Russisches Mönchtum, Entstehung, Entwicklung und*

Wesen, 988–1917. In: *Das östliche Christentum.* Abh., N. F., Heft 10/11. Würzburg, 1953.

——: *Das altrussische Mönchtum, Gestalter und Gestalten.* Würzburg, 1940.

For Chapter VII: Missionary Work and
the Spread of the Orthodox Church

BENZ, E., ed.: *Die Ostkirche und die russische Christenheit.* In Zusammenarbeit mit Hildegard Schaeder, L. Müller, R. Schneider. Tübingen, 1949.

——: "Leibniz und Peter der Grosse. Der Beitrag Leibnizens zur russischen Kultur—Religions—und Wirtschaftspolitik seiner Zeit." In: *Leibniz zu seinem 300. Geburtstag 1646–1946.* Berlin, 1947.

BONWETSCH, N.: *Cyrill und Methodius, die Lehrer der Slawen.* Erlangen, 1885.

BRÜCKNER, A.: *Die Wahrheit über die Slawenapostel.* 1913.

DVORNIK, FR.: *Les légendes de Constantin et de Méthode, vues de Byzance.* Prague, 1933.

GLAZIK, J.: "Die russisch-orthodoxe Heidenmission seit Peter dem Grossen." In: *Missionswissenschaftl. Abhandlungen und Texte,* ed. by Th. Ohm, OSB, Münster i. W., 1954.

GOSCHEW, I.: *Die heiligen Brüder Kyrillos und Methodius.* Sofia, 1937–38.

GRIVEC, F.: *Die heiligen Slawenapostel Cyrill und Method.* 1928.

LÜBECK, K.: "Die Christianisierung Russlands." *Abhandlungen aus Missionskunde und Missionsgeschichte,* Vol. 32, Aachen, 1922.

——: "Die russischen Missionen." The same, Vol. 33, Aachen, 1922.

SCHMIDT, K. D.: *Die Bekehrung der Ostgermanen zum Christentum. Der ostgermanische Arianismus.* Göttingen, 1939.

SCHUBERT, H. V.: *Die sogenannten Slawenapostel Cyrill und Method.* 1916.

VENYAMINOV, I.: *Wegweiser zum Himmelreich oder Vorfrage zur Belehrung der neugetauften Christen im russischen Amerika.* Odessa, 1848.

For Chapter VIII: Orthodox Culture

AMMANN, A. M.: *Untersuchungen zur Geschichte der kirchlichen. Kultur und des religiösen Lebens bei den Ostslawen.* Heft 1: *Die ostslawische Kirche im jurisdiktionellen Verband der byzantinischen Grosskirche (988–1459).* In: *Das östliche Christentum.* Abh., N. F., Heft 13. Würzburg, 1955.

ARSENIEW, N. V.: *Das heilige Moskau.* Paderborn, 1940.

BRÉHIER, L.: *Le monde byzantin: La civilisation byzantine.* Paris, 1950.

FEDOTOV, G. P.: *The Russian Religious Mind, Kievian Christianity.* Harvard, 1946.

GRATIEUX, A.: *A. S. Khomiakov et le mouvement slavophile.* Paris, 1939.

MASARYK, Th. G.: *Zur russischen Geschichts- und Religionsphilosophie.* Vols. I, II. Jena, 1913.

PORRET, E.: *Nikolaj Berdjajew und die christl. Philosophie in Russland.* Heidelberg, 1950.

RUSSACK, H. H.: *Byzanz und Stambul, Sagen und Legenden vom Goldenen Horn.* Berlin, 1941.

SCHESTOW, L.: *Athen und Jerusalem, Versuch einer religiösen Philosophie. Übertr. a. d. Russischen von H. Ruoff.* Graz, 1938.

TSCHIZEWSKIJ, DM.: *Altrussische Literaturgeschichte im 11, 12, und 13. Jahrhundert.* Frankfurt am Main, 1948.

For Chapter IX: The Ethical Ideas of Orthodoxy

BENZ, E.: "Menschenwürde und Menschenrecht in der Geistesgeschichte der Ostkirche." In: *Die Ostkirche und die russische Christenheit.* Tübingen, 1949.

SCHULTZE, SJ, B.: "Die Sozialprinzipien in der russischen Religionsphilosophie." In: *Zeitschrift f. kathol. Theologie*, Vol. 73, Heft 4, 1951.

WUNDERLE, G.: "Das Ideal der Brüderlichkeit in ostkirchlicher Sicht." In: *Sophia*. Dülmen, 1949.

For Chapter X: The Political Ideas of Orthodoxy

ANDERSON, P. B.: *People, State and Church in Modern Russia*. London, 1944.

BAYNES, N.: "Constantine the Great and the Christian Church." In: *The Proceedings of the British Academy*, Vol. 15, London, 1930.

GELZER, H.: "Das Verhältnis zwischen Staat und Kirche in Byzanz." In: *Ausgewählte kleine Schriften*. Leipzig, 1907.

GOETZ, L. K.: *Staat und Kirche in Altrussland*. Berlin, 1908.

KARTASCHOW, A.: "Die Entstehung der kaiserlichen Synodalgewalt unter Konstantin dem Grossen, ihre theologische Begründung und ihre kirchliche Rezeption." In: *Kirche und Kosmos, Orthod. u. Evang. Christentum, Studienheft*, No. 2, Witten-Ruhr, 1950.

KRUPNITZKIJ: *Die Theorie des dritten Rom*. 1952.

MEDLIN, W. K.: *Moscow and East Rome, a Political Study of the Relations of Church and State in Moscovite Russia*. Geneva, 1952.

OSTROGORSKY, G.: *Geschichte des byzantinischen Staates*. 2d ed. Munich, 1952.

PALMER, W.: *The Patriarch and the Tsar*. 6 vols. London, 1871–76.

SARKISYANZ, E.: *Russland und der Messianismus des Orients*. Tübingen, 1955.

SCHAEDER, HILDEGARD: *Moskau das dritte Rom*. Hamburg, 1929.

SCHMEMANN, A.: *Byzantine Theocracy and the Orthodox Church*. Geneva, 1948.

STÖKL, G.: "Die politische Religiosität des Mittelalters und die Entstehung des Moskauer Staates." In: *Saeculum,* Vol. II. 1951.

TREITINGER, O.: *Die oströmische Kaiser- und Reichsidee nach ihrer Gestaltung im höfischen Zeremoniell.* Jena, 1938.

ZAHN, Th.: "Konstantin der Grosse und die Kirche." In: *Skizzen aus dem Leben der Alten Kirche.* Erlangen and Leipzig, 1894.

ZERNOV, N.: *Moscow the Third Rome.* London, 1944.

For Chapter XI: Rome, Byzantium, Moscow

BOUSQUET: *L'unité de l'église et le schisme grec.* Paris, 1925.

BRÉHIER, ch.: *Le schisme oriental.* Paris, 1899.

DÖLGER, Fr.: "Rom in der Gedankenwelt der Byzantiner." In: *Zeitschrift für Kirchengeschichte,* Vol. 56, 1937.

DVORNIK, Fr.: *The Photian Schism. History and Legend.* Cambridge, 1948.

———: *Les Slaves, Byzance et Rome au IXe siècle.* Paris, 1926.

FLOROWSKIJ, A.: *Le conflit de deux traditions, la latine et la byzantine dans la vie intellectuelle de l'Europe orientale aux XVIe–XVIIe siècles.* Prague, 1937.

HARNACK, A. V.: *Der Geist der morgenländischen Kirche im Unterschied von der abendländischen.* Berlin, 1913.

HERGENRÖTHER, J.: *Photios, Patriarch von Konstantinopel, sein Leben, seine Schriften und das griechische Schisma.* 3 vols. 1867–69.

LEIB, B.: *Rome, Kiev et Byzance à la fin du XIe siècle.* Paris, 1924.

NORDEN, W.: *Das Papsttum und Byzanz. Die Trennung der beiden Mächte und das Problem ihrer Wiedervereinigung.* Berlin, 1903.

OHM, OSB, Th.: *Vom Christentum des Abendlandes, des Orients und der Zukunft.* Nuremberg, 1951.

PICHLER, A.: *Geschichte der kirchlichen Trennung zwischen dem Orient und Occident.* 2 vols. Munich, 1864–65.

PIERLING, SJ, P.: *La Russie et la Saint-Siège.* 3 vols. Paris, 1896–1901.

SCHULTZE, SJ, B.: *Russische Denker. Ihre Stellung zu Christus, Kirche und Papsttum.* Vienna, 1950.

SCOTT, S. H.: *The Eastern Churches and the Papacy.* London, 1928.

SEPPELT, F. X.: *Das Papsttum und Byzanz.* Breslau, 1904.

SPEMANN, Fr.: *Jerusalem, Wittenberg und Rom. Beiträge zur religiösen Frage der Gegenwart.* 2d ed. Barmen, 1910.

TYCIAK, J.: *Zwischen Morgenland und Abendland. Ein Beitrag zu einem west-östlichen Gespräch.* Düsseldorf, 1949.

ZHISHMAN, J.: *Die Unionsverhandlungen zwischen der orientalischen und der römischen Kirche seit dem Anfang des 4. Jahrhunderts bis zum Konzil von Ferrara.* Vienna, 1858.

For Chapter XII: Russia and Europe

BERDJAJEW, N.: *Christentum und Klassenkampf.* Lucerne, 1936.

——: *Sinn und Schicksal des russischen Kommunismus. Ein Beitrag zur Psychologie und Soziologie des russischen Kommunismus.* Lucerne, 1937.

DVORNIK, Fr.: *The Making of Central and Eastern Europe.* London, 1949.

JUST, A. W.: *Russland in Europa.* Stuttgart, 1949.

KIREJEWSKI, I. W.: *Russland und Europa.* Tr. and ed. with an afterword by N. v. Bubnoff. Stuttgart, 1948.

RAUCH, G. V.: "Moskau und der Westen." In: *Archiv für Kulturgeschichte,* Vol. XXXIV, Heft 1, Münster-Köln, 1951.

RIASANOVSKY, N. V.: *Russland und der Westen.* Munich, 1954.

SCHELTING, A.: *Russland und Europa im russischen Geschichtsdenken.* Bern, 1948.

SCHLOSSER, J. Fr. H.: *Die morgenländische und orthodoxe Kirche Russlands und das europäische Abendland.* Heidelberg, 1845.

For Chapter XIII: Orthodoxy within the Universal Church Today

ALIVISATOS, H. S.: "Orthodoxy, Protestantism and the World Council of Churches." In: *The Ecumenical Review,* Vol. 6, No. 3, April 1954.

BAUER, Br.: *Einfluss des englischen Quäkertums auf die deutsche Cultur und auf das englisch-russische Project einer Weltkirche.* Berlin, 1878.

BENZ, E.: *Wittenberg und Byzanz; zur Begegnung und Auseinandersetzung der Reformation und der Östlich-orthodoxen Kirche.* Marburg/L.: Elwert-Gräfe und Unzer, 1949.

———, and L. A. Zander, eds.: *Evangelisches und orthodoxes Christentum in Begegnung und Auseinandersetzung.* Hamburg, 1952.

BERDJAJEW, N.: "Die Krisis des Protestantismus u. d. russ. Orthodoxie." In: *Orient und Occident,* Vol. 1, 1929.

DOCUMENTS: "Les Églises orthodoxes et le mouvement oecuménique." In: *Istina,* Vol. 2, No. 2, April/June 1955.

———: "Le Patriarcat de Moscou et l'appel de l'assemblée d'Evanston." The same.

FLOROVSKY, G.: "The Eastern Orthodox Church and the Ecumenical Movement." In: *Theology Today,* Vol. 7, 1950.

KALOGIRU, J.: "Die orthodoxe Kirche im Lichte der ökumenischen Bewegung." In: *Internationale Kirchliche Zeitschrift,* 38 Jg., Heft 2, 1948.

KARMIRIS, J.: *The Orthodox Catholic Church and Her Re-*

lations with the Other Churches and with the World Council of Churches. Geneva, 1949.

MÜLLER, L.: "Das Gespräch zwischen Orthodoxen und Protestanten." In: *Osteuropa*, 2. Jg., Heft 2, April 1952.

———: *Die Kritik des Protestantismus in der russischen Theologie vom 16. bis zum 18. Jahrhundert. Akademie d. Wissenschaften u. d. Literatur in Mainz. Abh. d. Geistes- u. sozialwiss. Klasse,* Jg. 1951, Nr. 1.

———: *Russischer Geist und evangelisches Christentum.* Witten/Ruhr: *Luther-Verlag,* 1951.

ZANDER, L.: "The Ecumenical Movement and the Orthodox Church." In: *The Ecumenical Review,* Vol. 1, No. 3, Spring 1949.

Other publications by the author dealing with the Eastern Orthodox Church:

"Die Ostkirche im Lichte der protestantischen Geschichtsschreibung von der Reformation bis zur Gegenwart." In: *Orbis Academicus: Problemgeschichten der Wissenschaft in Dokumenten und Darstellungen,* Bd. 3, 1. Abt.: *Protestantische Theologie.* Freiburg/Munich, 1952.

Russische Heiligenlegenden. Übersetzt und erläutert von G. Apel, E. Benz, W. Fritze, A. Luther und D. D. Tschizewskij; hrsg. und eingeleitet von Ernst Benz. Zürich: Die Waage, 1953.

In addition, numerous articles in the *Zeitschrift für Kirchengeschichte* and the *Zeitschrift für Religions- und Geistesgeschichte.*